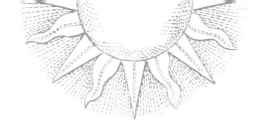

THE GREAT
HISPANIC HERITAGE

Isabel Allende

THE GREAT HISPANIC HERITAGE

THE GREAT
HISPANIC HERITAGE

Isabel Allende

Tim McNeese

CHELSEA HOUSE
PUBLISHERS
An imprint of Infobase Publishing

Isabel Allende

Copyright © 2006 by Infobase Publishing

Chelsea House
An imprint of Infobase Publishing
132 West 31st Street
New York NY 10001

Library of Congress Cataloging-in-Publication Data

McNeese, Tim.
  Isabel Allende / Tim McNeese.
     p. cm. — (The Great Hispanic heritage)
  Includes bibliographical references and index.
  ISBN 0-7910-8836-7 (hardcover)
  1. Allende, Isabel. 2. Authors, Chilean—20th century—Biography. I. Title. II. Series.
  PQ8098.1.L54Z78 2006
  863'.64—dc22   2006008379

Series design by Terry Mallon/Keith Trego
Cover design by Keith Trego

Printed in the United States of America

Bang EJB 10 9 8 7 6 5 4 3 2 1

This book is printed on acid-free paper.

Table of Contents

A Death
in the Family

Christmas was just a few weeks away, but Chilean writer Isabel Allende was distracted by other events. The year was 1991. A plane had brought her to Madrid, Spain, where she had traveled several other times during the previous decade. At one time, these flights had taken her away from her home in Venezuela. More recently, she had come from her California hillside home in San Rafael, outside San Francisco. The reason for each trip was almost always the same. She was being sent to a party hosted by a Spanish publisher in honor of her talents; one that was being held an ocean away from the place she called home. The purpose of each party was identical: to mark the publication of Isabel Allende's next novel.

This exiled woman from South America was a writer, someone who had finally found her voice on the pages of her works of fiction. She had spent her early years growing up in Chile, where her family had lived for hundreds of years. The daughter of a Chilean diplomat, Allende had lived in other parts of Latin America, but Chile

Isabel Allende was born in Peru and raised in Chile, although she was exiled from her Chilean homeland for years. As a successful writer, she has lived in many places throughout the world.

had always been home to her and her family, one that included grandparents, a loving yet fragile mother, and a daunting yet approachable stepfather whom she referred to as *Tio*, or "uncle." She had grown up, married, pursued a career in journalism, had two children, and created a life for herself, one in which she longed to play the role of a Latin American wife, while using her writing to challenge the entrenched chauvinism of Latin American men.

Isabel Allende did not mind all the traveling she had done in recent years, because the trips gave her an additional benefit: seeing her daughter. Her daughter, Paula, a lovely girl in her twenties, had moved to Spain, where she worked as a volunteer with underprivileged children. Allende was proud of her daughter and enjoyed her time with Paula more than the parties thrown in her honor. At the airport, Paula would be waiting, ready to see her mother, whose fame was growing with each of her books.

This time, however, when Allende reached the airport in Madrid, Paula was not there to meet her. Concerned, Allende found her hotel, left her suitcases in her room, and rushed to Paula's house. There, she found Paula struggling with a fever, nearly delirious. Paula's husband, Ernesto, described his wife's struggle over the previous weeks. She had begun to feel weak, so he had taken her to the emergency room of a nearby hospital. She had been treated for the flu and sent home. Ernesto explained that Paula had been feeling tired and frustrated. Allende and Ernesto worried that Paula might be suffering from depression as well as being sick. As best she could, Allende consoled her daughter.

Unable to do much more, Allende went on to her publisher's party. Dressed in an aubergine-colored dress and wearing a silver necklace with matching bracelets, she spoke to a crowd of well-wishers, fans, her publisher, and her literary agent and explained to them why she had written her most recent novel, one based on the flamboyant, exotic life of her American husband, a lawyer from northern California. All the while, Paula was still on her mind.

As Allende spoke at the party, her literary agent approached and whispered that Paula had been taken to the hospital. Allende left the party and rushed to be at her daughter's side, sprinting up six flights of stairs. Paula was suddenly much worse than she had been even the day before. Allende canceled the rest of her appointments, interviews, and appearances. The most difficult year of Allende's life was just beginning.

Allende's daughter, Paula, did not have the flu. She suffered from a disease called porphyria, an uncommon metabolic disorder that could lie dormant for years, but strike down its victims at any moment, poisoning him or her from within. The disease had attacked Paula with a vengeance.

Paula was taken to the hospital on December 6. Within just 48 hours, she had slipped into a coma. For the next year, from December 8, 1991, to December 8, 1992, Paula remained immobile, never waking, her body slowly wasting away. Allende remained near her daughter throughout that year of struggle and illness. There were endless tests and drugs, and a long line of doctors and specialists visited Paula. But the entire agonizing ordeal finally ended in Paula's death.

For Allende, Paula's fight with porphyria meant more than just a year lost in the corridors of hospitals and the personal darkness of an endless bedside vigil. She had lost her only daughter. How would she recover? How could she survive the death of her own child? Allende's mind began to wander into dangerous territory. She became depressed as she grieved for what was suddenly missing from her life. Allende felt like she had a huge cavern, a dark, empty void inside her, one that remained always cold and lifeless. She wondered about her own future as she tried to find a way to cope with the pain and tugging sense of abandonment. How could she ever write again? How could she even think of putting words on paper, knowing that none of them could bring back her daughter? She had flown from California to Madrid more than a year earlier as an internationally known author. Now, her daughter's death could bring an end to her spectacular literary life.

Memories
of Youth

LIFE IN LIMA

As Isabel Allende writes in her memoir *My Invented Country*, "I was born in Lima,"[1] the capital of Peru, on August 2, 1942. Despite the place of her birth, she was not Peruvian. Her parents were from Chile, and her father, Tomás Allende Pesce de Bilbaire, was serving as a diplomat at the Chilean Embassy in the Peruvian capital, so his daughter's birth took place in a foreign land.

Isabel's mother was Francisca Llona Barros. Although Isabel's father left his family when his daughter was very young, Isabel's mother remained her lifelong companion. She would become, Allende explained, "the most important person in my childhood, and she has been the most important person in my life."[2] Isabel's mother gave her daughter stability and love. "We laugh at the same things; we cry together, [and] we tell each other secrets. . . . Her love has always nourished me," writes Allende, "and I'm sure I wouldn't be who I am now without having had such an extraordinary relationship with her."[3]

Because her father was a diplomat who often had to bring his family to foreign countries, Isabel Allende was born in the city of Lima, Peru (pictured here), instead of in her parents' native Chile.

Allende's father got involved in international diplomacy and politics through his family, which was quite famous in Chile. His first cousin was Salvador Allende, who served as Chile's president from 1970 until 1973. (Salvador Allende had founded, with the help of other Chilean politicians, the Chilean Socialist Party in the 1930s.) Tomás Allende was of French origins on his mother's side. Regarding her blood heritage, Isabel Allende writes: "I have three-quarters Spanish-Basque blood, one-quarter French, and a bit of Araucan or Mapuche Indian, like everyone else in my land."[4] Tomás was highly intellectual, urbane, an unconventional man in a conventional Latin

American country, and a ladies' man. He was a man with a well-defined sense of humor who "was capable of making fun of his friends and of crushing his enemies with one witty, lapidary phrase."[5] He had met his future bride, Francisca, at a meeting of a literary society in Santiago, where "young literature buffs" came together to "discuss the works of the most famous Europeans of the period—Andre Gide, Malraux, Kafka, James Joyce, Virginia Woolf."[6] Once they married, Tomás and Francisca remained husband and wife for four years. During that time, which included two lengthy separations, Francisca gave birth to three children. Isabel was the first.

In her memoir *Paula*, published in 1994 and written about her daughter who died in 1992, Isabel Allende described her father, although her pictures of him came mainly from stories told to her by her mother and other relatives:

> My father had a taste for splendor. Ostentation had always been looked upon as a vice in Chile. . . . In contrast, in Lima, the city of viceroys, swagger and swash is considered stylish. Tomás installed himself in a house incommensurate with his position as second secretary in the embassy, surrounded himself with Indian servants, ordered a luxurious automobile from Detroit, and squandered money on parties, gaming, and yacht clubs, without anyone's being able to explain how he could afford such extravagances. . . . He became the indispensable element in Lima's revels. At the height of [World War II] he obtained the best whiskey, the purest cocaine, and the most obliging party girls; all doors opened to him.[7]

ABANDONMENT

Allende's father left home in 1945, when she was only three years old. She was so young when he left that she once claimed in an interview to "have no memory of my father."[8] But she was told stories of his departure and retold them in her 2003 memoir, *My Invented Country*:

Isabel Allende was always close to her mother, who is pictured here with her young children. Allende is on the right and her newborn brother, Francisco, is in his mother's arms.

My father went out to buy cigarettes and never came back. The truth is that he didn't start out to buy cigarettes, as everyone always said, but instead went off on a wild spree disguised as a Peruvian Indian woman and wearing bright petticoats and a wig with long braids. He left my mother in Lima with a pile of unpaid bills and three children, the youngest a newborn baby.[9]

Before Tomás Allende abandoned the family, he and young Isabel shared some time together. From her mother and others, she learned that her father "loved me very much,"[10] and that she would often sit on her father's lap as he showed her books, large volumes on art, and told her what he knew of well-known painters and artists. He talked to her about history, mythology, and storytelling. The two of them would sit, Isabel was told, and listen to classical music. But these memories, says Allende, are secondhand. As she explained, "[N]one of that

THE DEATH OF ISABEL ALLENDE'S FATHER

In her writings and interviews, Isabel Allende claims to have few, if any, real memories of her father. Since he abandoned his family when she was only three, she had not yet formed clear impressions of him. The stories of sitting on his lap and his showing her art books and speaking of history and mythology all come to her from her mother and other relatives. When her mother managed to get her marriage to Tomás Allende annulled, Isabel's father surrendered all paternal rights to his children. There would be no fatherly visitations. For three-year-old Isabel Allende, her father had vanished into thin air.

Allende admits it was not until she was in her fifties that she saw, for the first time, a photograph of her father as he would have looked when she was a young girl. Without this knowledge of her father's appearance, she found herself unable to identify him after his death. The story proved a difficult cross-roads for the daughter of a man who was, perhaps, the greatest mystery of her life.

When Allende was in her late twenties, Tomás Allende died of a heart attack in the streets of Santiago. After his body was taken to the local morgue, officials examined his papers and found his name to be Allende. They telephoned Isabel, assuming she might be a relative who could identify the body. As she hurried to the morgue, Allende thought the man on the coroner's table might be her brother Francisco "Pancho" Allende, whom stuck; classical music goes in one ear and out the other."[11] Despite being too young to remember these early literary influences, her father, in his own way, made attempts to introduce his daughter to the world of books.

After her husband abandoned the family, Isabel's mother packed up her three children and moved back to Chile. Francisca was just 25 years old. With few options available, she

she had not seen for several months. At the morgue, however, she found a much older man:

> ... when I arrived and they showed me the body, I could not identify it because I had never seen a picture of my father. It did not even occur to me that it could be my father. I never thought about my father. I did not know anything about him for twenty-eight years and I never thought it could be him. All I said was that it was not my brother.[*]

Unable to identify her father's body, Isabel called her stepfather, Ramon Huidobro, and asked him to come to the morgue. Once he arrived and viewed the mystery man's body, he turned to the daughter Tomas had abandoned decades earlier and said to her: "Isabel, this is your father."[**] With this last opportunity to be in the presence of her father, Isabel Allende discovered what she had known for years. The man on the table in front of her had no relevance in her life: "I took a good look and I did not feel any of what one could say is the call of the blood. I felt a total void."[***]

[*] Quoted in John Rodden, *Conversations with Isabel Allende* (Austin: University of Texas Press, 1999), 302.
[**] Ibid.
[***] Ibid.

had to "conquer the monumental pride with which she'd been brought up"[12] and ask permission to return to the home of her parents, Isabel's maternal grandparents.

But it was not easy. With the disappearance of her husband, Francisca was left with a stack of bills and little money to pay them. Allende later described her mother's situation: "She was alone in a strange land with three children, surrounded by the trappings of wealth but without a cent in her pocketbook and too proud to ask for help."[13] The Chilean government soon came to the rescue; because a Chilean official left his family, members of the government felt obligated to help Francisca and her children. The consul intervened, calling on the family and making it possible for them to come to Chile. The official who took care of the details for Francisca and her three children was Ramón Huidobro. He would one day marry Francisca and become Isabel's stepfather. In her later writings, Allende described Ramón as "a prince, and the direct descendant of Jesus Christ."[14]

With the move back to Chile, Francisca and her children left Peru behind. For young Isabel Allende, it was the end of a short chapter of her life that would be lost forever. As she has written: "My first years in Lima are obliterated in the mists of lost memory; all my recollections of childhood are linked to Chile."[15]

IN GRANDFATHER'S HOUSE

For most of the next decade, Isabel Allende's world centered around her family's native Chile, life in the capital city of Santiago, and living with her grandmother and grandfather. Her childhood world would later provide her with great inspiration for her writing. Allende grew up in a household dominated by her grandfather Agustin, as was common among Chilean families of that time. Agustin was the patriarch of the family, and he relished this role. He held strong opinions and beliefs and did not hesitate to make them known. His impact on young Isabel was dramatic:

My grandfather . . . was as solid and strong as a warrior, even though he was born with one leg shorter than the other. . . . He lived nearly a century with never a sign of a single loose screw. . . . On my desk I have a photograph of my grandfather. He looks like a Basque peasant. He's in profile, wearing a black beret that accentuates his aquiline nose and the firm expression of a face marked by deep furrows. He grew old strengthened by intelligence and reinforced by experience.

He died with a full head of white hair and blue eyes as piercing as those of his youth. . . . He spoke in proverbs, he knew hundreds of folk tales, and recited long poems from memory. This formidable man gave me the gift of discipline and love for language; without them I could not devote myself to writing today.[16]

Allende's grandfather had an extraordinary influence on her. Among other things, he tried to instill in his young granddaughter a love of Chile, her native country. She remembers him telling her to be a close observer of nature and "to love the landscape of Chile. He always said that just as Romans live among ruins and fountains without seeing them, we Chileans live in the most dazzling country on the planet without appreciating it."[17]

There were other influences on young Isabel as she grew up in the family mansion of her grandparents, a house that once stood on *Calle Suecia*, Number 081, but has since been turned into a dance club. There was her grandmother, whose influence was profound, but extremely different from that of her grandfather, Agustin. Isabel Barros Moreira was a self-proclaimed psychic and seer. Allende remembers this dominant aspect of her grandmother's life quite clearly:

My grandmother had extrasensory powers: she was half prophet, half clairvoyant, telepathic, and she could even move objects without touching them. She had a group of friends, the sisters Mora, who were quite famous at the time. They would

Isabel Allende's grandfather Agustin Llona Cuevas played a prominent role in her life. Allende spent many years of her childhood living in his home, where he taught her to cherish her native Chile.

get together with my grandmother and have spiritual séances. My grandmother did all this with a great sense of humor, openly, without allowing it to become macabre, solemn, or dark.[18]

She claimed the ability to make contact with spirits, including those of the dead. She told young Isabel that "space is filled with presences, the dead and the living all mixed together."[19] The elder Isabel had a keen sense of humor. She abhorred anything vulgar or crude. Allende remembered her adherence to "truth and justice that turned her into a hurricane when it came time to defend those principles."[20] Even today, Allende describes her grandmother as being her guardian angel, not only during the years of her childhood, but even now, decades after her death.

A WORLD OF BOOKS

Isabel Allende had other memories of living with her grandparents, her mother, and her two siblings in large mansions. She remembers how difficult it was to find a personal space growing up, with so many relatives and servants all around the mansion. But she enjoyed time alone, time spent playing by herself, when she created and told herself stories, saying them outloud. Reading was important to her, even as a young girl. But where could she find a quiet place to immerse herself in her books? At night, she would take a flashlight to bed and read under her bedcovers while everyone else was asleep. During the day, she scurried off to a special part of the big house, where no one else wanted to go, finding a quiet place for reading and play: the mansion's cellar.

The family cellar was a full excavation, taking up as much space as any other floor in the house. The adults kept the cellar door locked. But Isabel found her way in by crawling through a window. For light, she took candles out of the kitchen and brought along the flashlight she used to read under her bedsheets.

The cellar was made up of multiple rooms, all with dirt floors. It was "full of discarded objects, broken furniture, worn-out things, and ghosts."[21] Everywhere, the house's pipes and electrical wires ran under the ceiling beams, which Allende described as "all the bones of the house."[22] There, young Isabel found the quiet she was looking for. For most children, it would be a creepy place.

She was never truly alone. She remembers that spiders, roaches, and mice scurried everywhere. Isabel spent countless hours in the family cellar, finding new worlds in books and in her imagination. It would prove to be a special place where "Time was suspended . . . trapped in a bubble."[23] It was a world of her own making, one designed by a young girl,

> where I used to read by candlelight, dream of magic castles, dress up like a ghost, invent black masses, built forts out of an entire series of books that one of my uncles wrote about India, and then fall asleep among the spiders and mice. . . . A cavernous silence reigned and even my most tentative sigh sounded as strong as a gale. It was a beautiful world where the imagination knew no limits.[24]

The places she discovered through the printed page took Isabel around the world. In her subterranean reading room, she found a metal trunk stenciled with her father's initials, T. A. Inside, she discovered a stack of books that included works by Mark Twain, Jack London, Oscar Wilde, and George Bernard Shaw. She recalled the thrill of reading the nineteenth-century French science fiction writer Jules Verne's novel *20,000 Leagues Under the Sea*. She also enjoyed the novels of Emilio Salgari, *Sandokan's Revenge* and *The Black Corsair*.

Even as she was being introduced to the characters that filled the pages of the books she read, young Isabel transferred her literary discoveries into her own form of storytelling. She began to tell stories to her brothers, Pancho and Juan. Her ability to spin tales was so well defined at an early age, that the two boys would only have to say one word, "like 'squirrel' or 'star,' and [she] would launch into a tale about the squirrel or star, to the delight of her attentive listeners."[25]

Isabel had other interests besides reading, of course. She and her brothers played games and climbed trees. But Isabel loved her time alone, taking the characters of fiction she discovered in the pages of books and transferring them from their two-dimensional place on the page to the three-dimensional world of theater. She would create figures fashioned out of toothpicks and act, placing the figures on her own miniature stage. She would speak for them, give them dialogue as "she breathed life into inanimate objects."[26] This first flirtation with childhood theater would begin a lifelong interest in creating worlds filled with characters of her own making.

3

Other Worlds

A NEW FATHER

It was all so much child's play. They were, after all, just children. But Isabel Allende's childhood was no simple experience. It was preparatory. It was all part of creating Isabel Allende the writer. There were games and secret places and wild imaginings. There were special people—a loving mother, a spiritualist grandmother, and a Chilean grandfather who guided with a strict hand, yet gave of himself to his family. It was not perfect. As Isabel Allende described it: "My childhood wasn't a happy one, but it was interesting."[27]

The six years between her father's abandonment and her family's departure from the hacienda of Agustin and Isabel were wondrous years, years of growth and experience, learning and love, drama and departure, maternalism and memories. "And no one can live without memories,"[28] Allende has written. The impact of those years spent under her grandparents' roof stayed with her throughout the rest of her adult years until, by the early 1980s, through inspiration she gained as a child—the great hacienda, her spiritualist grandmother, her loving mother, the storytelling, the blood memories—she would pen her first novel, *The House of the Spirits*.

Memories and departure provided the bookends of Isabel's early youth. The day came when it was time for her mother to create a new life for herself, one outside the confines of her mother and father's hacienda. The Chilean official, Ramón Huidobro, the one who had rescued Isabel's family from poverty in the name of the Chilean government, rescued them a second time. This time, it was not as a bureaucrat, but as a man in love with Isabel's mother, Francisca. As Isabel remembers, Huidobro was the ugliest of all the men who were interested in her mother. Despite his appearance, their love provided Isabel with her last memory spent in the shadowy, candle-lit cellar of her early youth: "I was nine years old when I left my childhood home and with great sadness said good-bye to my unforgettable grandfather."[29]

Just as Tomás Allende had detached himself from his family, forever altering all their lives, another man entered their lives and became the father Isabel Allende had never known.

LIFE WITH "TIO"

After he managed to get Isabel's mother and the children back to Chile, Huidobro stayed in Lima, always keeping in touch with the Allende family. He remained in government service, receiving assignments that took him out of the country, to Peru, then Bolivia. All the time, he was intent on pursuing a relationship with Isabel's mother. Whenever he was away working in a foreign office, he and Francisca exchanged letters. He tried to get an annulment from his wife. Francisca received her own annulment quickly, but, according to Isabel: "Tio Ramón, in contrast, has never, not to this day, succeeded in annulling his first marriage."[30] He left his wife anyway, and he and Francisca were "married" when Isabel was nine years old.

Although Isabel Allende's mother, Francisca, remarried, she always spent a great deal of time with her children. She and young Isabel are pictured here in a photograph taken in 1950.

Under these circumstances, the beautiful Francisca was soon marked by Chilean society as "the other woman," one who had stolen a husband away from his wife. Isabel's mother—and sometimes Isabel and her brothers, too—endured stares and harsh words from people who considered Francisca immoral. Despite these difficult encounters, Ramón Huidobro brought a new life to Francisca and the children. As Allende later explained:

> He was my true father. We traveled widely with him and he was the one who formed me. I owe him my intellectual inquisitiveness, my curiosity, and my discipline. . . . He had a Jesuit upbringing, and somehow he transmitted that: the dialectic, the rigor, the ability to set a goal and walk straight towards it. He has been the only person in my life with whom I can talk about absolutely everything and without a mask: sex, money, sin, work. I can talk about those topics without worrying about hurting or bothering him.[31]

Huidobro's presence helped create new memories for Isabel. He had a car, a Ford, which was actually only half his, since he bought it with a friend. Huidobro had the car on Mondays, Wednesdays, Fridays, and every other Sunday. On those Sundays, he would take the family out for drives in the country. Isabel recalls one drive to a rural area near a mental institution for nonviolent patients called The Open Door. Huidobro had grown up with his family vacationing with relatives who farmed the institution's surrounding fields and orchards. At one of the orchards near the mental facility, Huidobro took the children, and soon Isabel and her siblings were clambering up in the branches of apricot trees heavy with fruit. Some of the patients came out to greet the family, and the children cowered in fear. But Huidobro knew many of the patients by name and spoke to them, assuring the children that there was nothing to be afraid of. The family picked apricots, the children tossed them at one another in play, and each child ate his or her fill until their stomachs cramped. Even though the day might not have seemed special to Isabel's stepfather, she remembered it well:

We ate till we could eat no more, then kissed our new friends goodbye and piled into the old Ford for the return trip, continuing to stuff ourselves from the overflowing bag of fruit. . . . That day, for the first time ever, I realized that life can be generous. I had never experienced anything similar with my grandfather, or any other member of my family, all of whom believed that paucity is a blessing and avarice a virtue. . . . My grandfather had a fortune, but I never suspected that until much later. Tio Ramon was poor as a church mouse, but I didn't know that either, because he always showed us how to enjoy the little we had. At the most difficult moments of my life . . . the taste of those apricots comes back to me with the notion that abundance is always within reach, if only one knows how to find it.[32]

Unlike other people or family members connected to Isabel Allende's life, her stepfather cannot be found directly in her novels. When asked why, she explained: "[B]ecause he has common sense. People who have common sense are not good protagonists for novels, but they are fantastic to live with."[33]

A NEW LIFE ABROAD

By the time of Francisca's marriage to Ramón Huidobro, Allende's grandmother had died. The blow was crushing because her grandmother was special, with unique powers. Her death left Isabel's grandfather crushed and he never recovered from the loss.

By the time Isabel turned 11, her life was a whirlwind of new places and schools. Her stepfather, through his work in the Chilean diplomatic service, was assigned to Bolivia, where the family took up residence in the capital city of La Paz. The assignment came close on the heels of Isabel's grandmother's death. Isabel remembers the move to her new Latin American home, which consisted of automobile trips with suitcases tied up on top of the car, a voyage by ship to a foreign port, and

Isabel Allende's stepfather's work as a diplomat took him to cities through-out the world. When Isabel was 11, her family moved to La Paz, Bolivia, which is pictured here.

finally reaching their destination on a narrow-gauge train "that climbed toward the heights of Bolivia at the pace of a mil-lenarian snail."[34] The move meant leaving her grandfather behind, and she later recalled the scene and its significance: "The sight of my grandfather . . . with his cane and his Basque beret . . . standing at the door of the house where I grew up marked the end of my childhood."[35]

Life in La Paz had its own magic and brought a new life to Isabel. The mountain city was so high in elevation and the air so thin that, as Allende writes, "you can see the angels at dawn."[36] The family lived in a compound that held two other houses and families who all shared a garden. These common grounds became a new sanctuary for Isabel, where she "sought solitude and silence in the paths of that large garden."[37] She attended a coeducational school, where she came into contact with a great number of boys for the first time. Isabel ran afoul of her teacher quickly. One of her class's first history lessons cast Chilean soldiers in the nineteenth century as having committed atrocities against Peruvian and Bolivian troops. Isabel was outraged, having been taught that her nation's fighting men were brave patriots. When she tried to defend her nation's reputation, she was "greeted by a hail of spitballs."[38]

The teacher sent her from the room, ordering Isabel to stand in a corner in the hallway. Angry and hurt, she soon noticed a boy who was being punished in the opposite corner of the hall. According to Allende, two major events occurred in the hall. She experienced, perhaps for the first time in her life, "love at first sight."[39] Second, Isabel felt her hormones flaring, signaling the onset of her first menstrual period. It was a day worthy of mention in her memoi, *Paula*. As for the boy, the object of her first school-girl crush, Isabel recalled that he "treated me with such indifference that I came to believe I was invisible in his presence."[40]

A POSTING IN BEIRUT

Fortunately for Isabel, who was a target of ridicule at school, the family's stay in La Paz was not a long one. Tío Ramón received a new diplomatic assignment, this time in Beirut, Lebanon, two continents and a great ocean to the east. The year was 1955 and this move was even more dramatic than the relocation from Santiago to La Paz. Francisca packed up her children again and, as Huidobro flew alone to Paris, then to Lebanon, the family rode another train, this time down a mountain. While on the mountain train, Francisca and her children traveled under the protection of a local Indian carrying an out-of-date rifle, "who never slept but crouched on the floor chewing coca leaves."[41] Francisca was afraid he would turn on them at any moment and kill them all, so she told her children to stay alert throughout the entire train trip. From a Chilean port, Isabel and her family took passage on an Italian ocean liner that delivered them to Genoa, Italy. Then they took a bus ride to Rome.

Isabel's brother Juan caused a stir onboard the ship when, during a game of hide-and-seek, he fell asleep in one of the ship's unused staterooms. When he could not be found, the ship's captain prepared to lower lifeboats to search for him in the waters of the Atlantic. Fortunately, a ship's whistle woke Juan up before the search began. As for Isabel, she "fell in love with all the sailors with a passion nearly as violent as that inspired by my young Bolivian, but I suspect they had eyes only for my mother."[42] They completed their two-month-long journey on a plane that landed in Beirut.

Tio Ramón and his family remained in Beirut for three years, and the teenage Isabel faced new adventures and difficulties in her new Middle Eastern home. It was extremely hot in Beirut, "very different from [the climate] of Chile."[43] The family lived in a tiny apartment. Letters to and from Chile took months to arrive. Huidobro did not make much money and expenses were always tight, making a trip to the movies or to an ice-skating rink a luxury. There was also the problem of language. In Lebanon, people spoke French and Arabic, and Isabel and her brothers struggled to learn these languages well enough to speak to people on the streets. It was a time of insecurity for Isabel, especially after the arrival of one of Huidobro's own daughters who was close to her age. Isabel became frightened that she would lose her mother's love to this other girl.

Life in Beirut was beyond exotic for Isabel. The city was beautiful and modern, considered the "Paris of the Middle East." Isabel soon realized that her new home was a multicultural world filled with wonderful contrasts:

[T]raffic was tied up by camels and sheikhs' Cadillacs with gold bumpers and Muslim women, draped in black with only a peephole for their eyes, shopped in the souks elbow to elbow with scantily clad foreigners. On Saturdays, some of the housewives in the North American colony liked to wash their cars wearing shorts and bare midriff tops. Those Arab men who rarely saw women without veils came from remote villages, harrowing journeys by burro, to attend the spectacle of the half-naked foreign women. The locals rented chairs and sold coffee and syrupy sweets to the spectators lined up in rows on the opposite side of the street.[44]

Isabel attended an English school for girls, which was run by a Miss St. John. The goal of the school was to instill discipline and build character. Isabel had to wear a blue uniform that she hated, along with "orthopedic-looking shoes and a pith helmet–style hat pulled down to our eyebrows, an outfit that would take the wind out of anyone's sails."[45] The school food was a daily ration of rice served with either vegetables, yogurt, or boiled liver.

Since the school was a boarding institution, Isabel's classmates came from all over the world. The curriculum included learning English and studying the Bible. The future novelist remembers memorizing and reciting an endless litany of Bible verses. Isabel recalls that between Bible lessons, she and the other girls giggled and talked about the new American rock-and-roll singer Elvis Presley, "whom none of us had seen or heard but who was said to create havoc with his electric guitar and rotating pelvis."[46] Each day at school was longer for Isabel than for any of the other students. Since she did not live there, she came and went by bus, and she was "the first to be picked up in the morning and the last to be left off in the afternoon."[47]

GROWING UP

Eventually, among the increasing turmoil of Lebanese and Middle Eastern politics, the city of Beirut became a dangerous place. Violence and insurrection, fueled by a developing and heated Arab nationalism, rocked the city, and its streets became a battleground. To restore peace, U.S. President Dwight Eisenhower dispatched U.S. Marines onboard the Navy's North American 6th Fleet in 1958, and the Marines were sent in to restore order to the city. Isabel continued to ride

Isabel Allende and her family were living in Beirut, Lebanon, during a period of turmoil in the Middle East. In 1958, U.S. Marines were sent to the area to help bring order to the city after Lebanese Muslims rebelled against the standing government.

the bus to school, because Miss St. John was able to get permission for it to pass through the Marine checkpoint. But the ride was dangerous, and Isabel remembers hearing machine gun fire and "through dense smoke, one could glimpse the bodies of the fallen."[48] Parents removed their children from the school and the seats of classrooms emptied until Miss St. John was forced to close the school. By then, her only student was Isabel Allende.

Isabel was maturing, growing from a girl into a woman. She attended her first coed dance and moved to the rhythm of

A DANCE AND A KISS, AMERICAN STYLE

While living in Beirut, 15-year-old Isabel was invited to a dance held at the U.S. Embassy, hosted by the U.S. ambassador and his wife. Frightened of going to a party with strangers and uncertain of her dancing ability, Isabel did not want to go at first, but Tío Ramón talked her into it, telling her: "Remember that all the others are more afraid than you."* To bolster his stepdaughter's courage, Ramón closed the Chilean consulate early the day before the dance to teach her several dance steps. Isabel remembers the afternoon fondly: "With single-minded tenacity, he made me sway to the rhythm of the music, first holding the back of a chair, then a broom, and finally him. In several hours I learned everything from the Charleston to the samba."**

Her first kiss came not long after her first dance. During the summer of 1958, U.S. troops entered Beirut in response to a rebellion caused by Lebanese Muslims. From her apartment building, Isabel could see fighting in the street.

Soon after the Americans arrived, "greeted with a salvo of applause"*** from the people of Beirut, Isabel met some of them while they were off-duty at a local ice skating rink. There were hundreds of young American soldiers in their uniforms, who all looked alike to the teenage Isabel, with their short hair and tattoos. She spoke to some of them, trying to understand their style of English. From one of them she received her first kiss: "[I]t was like biting a frog that smelled of chewing gum, beer, and tobacco. I have no idea which one kissed me . . . they all looked alike—but I do remember that from that very moment I decided to explore the matter of kisses."†

    * Isabel Allende, *Paula* (New York: HarperCollins Publishers, 1994), 68.
  ** Ibid.
 *** Ibid., 86.
   † Ibid.

rock and roll. She discovered the classic book *A Thousand and One Nights*. It was within the pages of this Arab classic that Isabel became lost

> in magical tales of princes on flying carpets, genies in oil lamps, and appealing thieves who slipped into the sultan's harem disguised as old ladies to indulge in marathon love fests with forbidden women with hair black as night, pillowy hips and breasts like apples, soft women smelling of musk and eager for pleasure.[49]

Through the three years Tio Ramón and his family lived in Beirut, Isabel Allende had blossomed into a young woman, one who was curious about the rest of the world and of love. It was there, through a prism of extraordinary sights and experiences, that Isabel filed away images of places and people that she would later resurrect in her fiction.

Inventing
Her World

HOME TO GRANDFATHER

With the violence expanding in the Middle East in the late 1950s, Tio Ramón and Isabel's mother, Francisca, decided that there were safer places to raise their children. Officials in Lebanon were warning foreign diplomats to send their families out of the country. Even the U.S. Marines received orders to return to their ships and leave the Middle East. Isabel and her brothers were soon placed onboard one of the last commercial flights out of violence-torn Beirut. They were bound for Chile and their grandfather's house. On the plane, Isabel wrote a letter to her mother, uncertain when she would see her again. (Within a few months, Ramon was reassigned, and he and Francisca made their way out of Lebanon to Turkey.) She could not know that she and her mother "were going to be separated for most of the remainder of our lives."[50]

Once the children were back in Chile, Isabel's grandfather decided that she had gone far enough in school. She was, after all, 15 years old, and, as she would admit in her memoirs, "up till then, my education had been chaotic. . . . I lacked the most elemental knowledge for functioning in the world."[51] Her grandfather said he would take personal responsibility for teaching Isabel geography and history. (Although she had lived in Lebanon, she was unable to locate the Middle Eastern country on a map.) The lessons with her grandfather did not come easy for either of them, but, as with any good schooling, it had its rewards:

> He taught me history and geography, showed me maps. Made me read Chilean writers, corrected my grammar and handwriting. As a teacher, he was short on patience but long on severity; my errors made him red with anger, but if he was content with my work he would reward me with a wedge of camembert cheese, which he ripened in his armoire; whenever he opened that door, the odor of stinking army boots flooded the neighborhood.[52]

Isabel Allende and her grandfather spent some of their best times together after her return to his household as a teenager. They enjoyed sitting in the same room, not necessarily talking but just being together, "reading or watching the rain drum against the windowpanes. . . . I believe we had a mutual liking and respect for one another."[53] There were also times when the two shared conversation. The old man took the opportunity to tell his granddaughter the things he wanted her to know. Their time together made Isabel appreciate her heritage: "I think I fell in love with my country because of the stories my grandfather told me."[54]

It soon became clear that Isabel's mathematics skills were lacking, so her grandfather placed her in private math classes taught by a "tiny old lady with jet-dyed hair and several missing teeth."[55] The math teacher had only five students besides Isabel. Isabel soon started to like one of them. The young man always sat by her, shared his math notes, and walked with her to the bus each day. They went to the movies together and watched a horror film featuring a man-sized, underwater creature with fins that menaced unsuspecting female swimmers. The two teens held hands in the darkened theater, and Isabel returned to her grandfather's house certain that "I had met the love of my life and that our intertwined hands signified a formal engagement."[56] She was wrong. Eventually, the boy stopped attending the math tutoring sessions. Another young love had slipped away.

MEETING MICHAEL

Another, more permanent love came Isabel's way when she was in her late teens. She was introduced to Michael Frias by a mutual friend. Frias was the son of British parents. His family had lived in Chile for several generations but "still call[ed] England 'home.'"[57] His father worked for a North American copper company in the northern region of Chile. His family lived in a neighborhood with other people from England. They had "air conditioning, bottled water, and a profusion of catalogs from which they could order from the United States anything from condensed milk to terrace furniture."[58] Michael had grown up with few contacts outside this little English world. When Isabel met him, he was 20 years old and had just begun to study civil engineering. She described him:

> He rode a motorcycle and lived in an apartment with a housekeeper who treated him like a young lord; he never washed a pair of socks or boiled an egg. He was tall, young, handsome, and very slender, with large caramel-colored eyes. And he blushed when he was nervous. . . . He came to see me one day under the pretext of helping me with my chemistry, and soon asked formal permission from my grandfather to take me to the opera. We went to see *Madame Butterfly*. . . . That was the beginning of a long, sweet courtship destined to last many years before being consummated. . . . It was several months

before we held hands . . . and almost a year before our first kiss.[59]

Michael Frias became Isabel's first real boyfriend. She later wrote about how, when he "asked me to be his girlfriend . . . I was so desperate that I latched onto him like a crab and never let go."[60]

Isabel's relationship with the young man who would eventually become her husband began with a slow rhythm of innocence and happy discovery. There were conversations in the house of her grandfather, who watched the young couple closely as they enjoyed "cups of tea in the winter and ice cream in the summer."[61] Michael took Isabel on a motorcycle ride once a week to a music concert. On every other Saturday, she was allowed to go with Michael to the movies. Her grandfather liked the young college student. He invited Michael to family dinners on Sunday, an invitation that was understood to be a significant sign of acceptance. "I like this young man," the family patriarch told Isabel. "He is going to improve the race."[62]

Isabel remembers well her first meeting with Michael's parents. They were on a visit to Santiago, and Michael took her to a traditional English five o'clock tea, complete with special porcelain cups and wonderful cakes, all laid out on a starched tablecloth. It was all so British. Michael's parents were pleasant to the young Isabel, even gracious. They appeared to like her, and she was soon caught up in their hospitality:

I felt they had accepted me even before they met me, grateful for the love I showered on their son. . . . Michael's mother charmed me from the moment I met her; she was an innocent, incapable of a mean thought; her goodness glowed in her liquid aquamarine eyes. She accepted me without reservation, as if we had known each other for years. Both of Michael's parents must have wished for their son a calm, discreet girl from the English colony. . . . It is, therefore, all the more admirable that they opened their arms to me so promptly.[63]

Isabel Allende and her husband, Michael, actually had two weddings—one a civil ceremony and the other a religious ceremony.
She is pictured here in her wedding gown, with her brothers Juan
(left) and Francisco.

It was yet another important step in a wonderful and
lengthy courtship for Isabel and Michael. Five years after they
met, they were married.

A WORKING WOMAN

Isabel finished her special studies and graduated at the age of
17. At the time, she had no idea what she wanted to do as a

career. In fact, the idea of working was something she had not really taken seriously. She had always assumed she would get married and have children, "because that was what girls did in those days."[64] But the timing was not yet right for marriage. Michael still had several years left before he would finish his studies. Knowing her daughter better than anyone else, Isabel's mother suggested that Isabel continue her own studies, perhaps focus on theater. But no sooner had Isabel finished school than she landed her first real job.

Without any college study or specialized training on her résumé and being only 17 years old, Isabel assumed that she would have few job options. She intended to find work as a secretary. She had heard, however, that jobs connected with the United Nations (UN) paid fairly well, and she could speak both English and French. While searching for a listing for the UN in the phone directory, Isabel found a number and address for a UN agency called FAO. Uncertain what the initials even stood for (it was the Food and Agricultural Organization), she went to the address. In her meeting with a low-level UN bureaucrat, she learned the name of the official in charge of the agency—Don Hernan Santa Cruz, who was away in Europe. She was sent on to the next highest ranking official for an interview. When she arrived, she led the young Italian official to believe that she had been sent by his boss, Santa Cruz. She was hired on the spot, although "I had presented the lowest score on the typing exam of anyone in the history of the Food and Agricultural Organization."[65] (As for her ruse of knowing Santa Cruz, it caught up with her a month later when the UN official returned to the Chilean office. When Isabel explained herself, the official was amused. Fortunately, he had been one of Tomás Allende's closest boyhood friends.)

Isabel was assigned first as a secretary to an Argentine forestry expert. She found the job terribly boring. Much of her time was spent copying forestry statistics. Then, she was moved to the Department of Information. To earn more money, Allende took a second, part-time job translating popular romance novels from English to Spanish. The subject matter of the romances rankled Isabel. The plots were all the same: "beautiful, innocent, and penniless young girl meets mature, strong, powerful, virile, and lonely man disappointed in love in some exotic setting, for example, a Polynesian island where she works as a governess and he owns a plantation."[66] Sometimes, driven by an early feminist urge, Allende would make changes as she translated the novels, intent on making the innocent heroines appear stronger and more decisive. After only a few months, she was fired.

Although Isabel Allende was not "officially" introduced to the subject of feminism until the mid-1960s, even at 16 and 17 years of age, she was painfully aware that the world was divided into two hemispheres: male and female. Women had to live up to certain expectations from which men were exempt. When she graduated from school, she did not expect to attend college. Her mother, stepfather, and grandfather did not expect her to continue her education, either. It was assumed that her two brothers, however, would go to institutions of higher learning. It was the way the world worked at the time. Women did not become professionals. They married and had children. In later years, as a practicing feminist, Isabel Allende looked back at it all with greater understanding:

> The daughters of certain emancipated or intellectual families went to the university, but that was not true for me. . . . It was expected that my brothers would be professional men—if possible doctors or engineers . . . but I was to settle for a largely decorative job until motherhood occupied me completely. . . . That has changed, I'm happy to say, and today the level of education for women is actually higher than for men. I wasn't a bad student. But since I already had a boyfriend it didn't occur to anyone that I might go to the university—not even to me.[67]

In the meantime, her mother and stepfather had returned from Turkey, and Isabel was once again living under their roof.

The years she had spent living with her grandfather had become precious to her and, even as she moved out of his house, Isabel continued to visit him almost daily, usually on her way home from work each evening.

A PROFESSIONAL LIFE

Isabel remained at the Department of Information for several years. It was there that she came under the tutelage of a couple of journalists "who taught me to write in Spanish because I hardly knew it. I had had a very uneven education in French, English, and a bit of Spanish."[68] She learned how to write and do the job of a journalist. It was through this training that Allende first got into television, taking a job where she presented a weekly program that was offered by the United Nations in Chile through public access television.

As Isabel's professional life was slowly taking shape, her personal life was moving ahead as well. At age 19, after having dated for several years, she and Michael were married. Since Michael was still in engineering school, it was understood that they would have to live on Isabel's salary alone. They sat down together "with paper and pencil and came to the conclusion that two people could subsist, barely, on my salary, and that it would be worth taking a chance."[69] Their decision was enthusiastically greeted by Isabel's mother, who excitedly sold the Persian rug from the family living room as start-up money for her daughter's wedding fund.

There would be two weddings. Isabel and Michael were first married in a civil ceremony on a pleasant day in the spring of 1962 at her parents' large colonial hacienda. It was "an intimate gathering attended only by our two families—that is, nearly a hundred people."[70] The future president of Chile, Isabel's uncle Salvador Allende, was there. He gave away the bride in the absence of Tomás, her long vanished father. A week later, Allende and Michael were married again in a church ceremony, "even though Michael was Anglican and I was no longer a practicing Catholic, because the weight of the Church in the world I was born into is like a millstone around one's neck."[71] This time, Tio Ramón walked Isabel down the aisle. On the way to the reception, the newly married couple's car blew a tire, and Isabel watched as her husband took off his formal jacket to help the car's chauffeur change the flat.

At first, Allende and Michael lived in her parents' house. Tio Ramón had been assigned to a diplomatic post in Switzerland, leaving the house available for the newlyweds. But the house was too big for just the two of them and, after suffering several robberies (the house sat all day with no one at home while Isabel worked and Michael attended school), they moved into her grandfather's house, which was now vacant, since he had retired and moved to a family beach house. Isabel and Michael soon settled into married life.

Seasons in the Sun

PIONEERING WOMAN

Isabel Allende soon fell into a busy world that required her to strike a balance between her domestic married life and her budding professional career. She was developing into a television reporter while still working for the United Nations. Journalism was her new calling, along with her husband, Michael. She developed a passion for television work, although she had never taken a single journalism course in college:

> In those days, journalism was still a profession you learned on the job, and there was a certain tolerance for spontaneous practitioners like me. . . . My grandfather was indignant when I told him what I was doing; he considered reporting an occupation for knaves; no one of sound mind would talk with the press, and no decent person would choose a calling in which the main order of work was talking about other people. However, I think he secretly watched my

television programs because occasionally he let slip some revealing comment.[72]

These were pioneering steps for a woman in early 1960s Chile. Today, by contrast, most Chilean journalists are women. By the 1970s, Isabel had become one of the most recognized female television personalities in Chile.

THE MAKING OF A TELEVISION PERSONALITY

Isabel Allende found her way into television during the medium's earliest days in Chile. Originally, Chilean television consisted of a pair of university-based channels that broadcast in black-and-white. Only the privileged could afford to buy a television. But once an individual owned a television, he or she became quite influential. Television owners often hosted neighbors who ". . . spent entire afternoons, openmouthed, eyes glazed, awaiting some revelation that would change the course of their lives,"[*] as they stared into the television screens.

Allende entered the world of broadcasting almost by accident, but her first effort immediately paid off. The channel's producer spoke to Allende following her first 15-minute broadcast and "with a sigh of resignation, asked me to come back every Wednesday to campaign against hunger—the poor man was frantic to fill his schedule."[**] It had all happened so haphazardly, but it proved to be the beginning of a television career for Allende that would last for many years and made her one of the most recognized women in Chile.

* Isabel Allende, *Paula* (New York: HarperCollins Publishers, 1994), 131.
** Ibid.

As for her domestic life, she became pregnant within the first year of her marriage and gave birth to her first child, daughter Paula, on October 22, 1963. Despite Allende's budding feminism, she worked hard to satisfy her husband and comply with his wishes, "selfless and servile as a geisha,"[73] as was expected of a Chilean wife of the 1960s:

> I ran the house, I looked after the children, and I ran like a marathoner the whole day to fight my way through the pile of responsibilities that had fallen on me, including a daily visit to my grandfather, but at night I waited for my husband with the olive for his martini between my teeth and the clothing he would wear the next morning carefully laid out.[74]

OFF TO EUROPE

Within a couple of years of their marriage, Michael finished his engineering studies and graduated. But neither Allende nor her husband were content to live out a typical Chilean marriage. They both wanted to see more of the world. They applied for special government funding and both obtained scholarships for study and work abroad. With little Paula not yet two years old, the family moved to Europe. Soon, they were splitting their time between Switzerland and Belgium. In the Belgian city of Brussels, they lived in a small attic apartment over a barbershop. They were poor, dependent on money from the government, "but we were in our twenties, an age when poverty is fashionable."[75]

Michael studied engineering, and Isabel studied television journalism in a university course. Since the scholarship she received had also been offered to would-be students from the African Congo, she took classes with young African men. There she was, "a light-skinned woman among thirty black males."[76] The experience left Isabel with two overarching insights: the impact of reverse discrimination and exposure to African male chauvinism.

The clash of race, culture, and the sexes was extraordinary. The African men considered women second-class citizens and were rude to Allende. After only a week, Isabel tried to drop out of the course, explaining to her director that "in my country men did not enter the women's bathroom unzipping their fly, did not shove women aside to go through a door first, did not knock each other down for a place at the table or to get on a bus, and that I . . . was leaving because I was not used to such foul behavior."[77] Ironically, the Africans were equally appalled at Allende's behavior, since no woman in their country would ever try to go through a door before a man, but, instead, always walked behind. Between them, they came to an agreement. She agreed to walk several steps behind them, never raise her voice in class, and let the men go through doors ahead of her. In exchange, "they stopped bursting into the bathroom and physically shoving me."[78] This demeaning experience brought Allende further into the fold of feminism.

Despite such difficulties, Isabel and Michael enjoyed their time on the European continent. By scrimping and saving, they managed to save enough money to travel "from Andalusia to Oslo in a broken-down Volkswagen . . . that sneezed along the highway with all our goods and chattel strapped to the roof."[79] They slept in a tent by night and, by day, "poked through countless castles, cathedrals, and museums, carrying [Paula] in a backpack and feeding [her] Coca-Cola® and bananas."[80]

RETURN TO CHILE

In 1966, Isabel, Michael, and three-year-old Paula left Europe and returned to Chile. Allende was pregnant with her second child. Although they had only been away from Chile for a few years, things were different. Politically, the country was under a new regime, as the Christian Democrats had won a majority in the Parliamentary elections the previous year. At the time, this did not bode well for Isabel's uncle Salvador Allende, a major political figure and leader of the Chilean Socialist Party, which

In 1962, Isabel Allende married Michael Frias and the couple had two children—Paula, born in 1963, and Nicolás, born in 1966. This photograph of Nicolás and Paula was taken in 1969.

he had helped establish more than 30 years earlier. (He served as president of the Chilean Senate from 1965 until 1969.) Many people in Chile were already suggesting that Allende and the members of his political party would soon lose favor. However, these predictions were proven wrong in just a few years.

Meanwhile, in Santiago, Isabel and Michael found a small enclave of hippies "in their Indian prints, necklaces, flowers, and long hair."[81] Hippies were new to Chile, but Allende and Michael had seen them throughout Europe. At the time, Isabel had no patience for the "bucolic indolence of the Flower Children,"[82] but she did like the long dresses worn by hippie girls and she fell in love with flowers, painting them on the walls of her home and on the family car: "enormous yellow sunflowers and bright dahlias that scandalized my in-laws and our neighbors."[83] There were other changes, too, after Isabel gave birth to a son, Nicolás.

Journalism remained important to Isabel, and she soon found new outlets for her writing. She had changed just as much as Chile had in her absence. Her interest in feminism had developed further. In 1965, while living in Switzerland, Isabel had met a fellow Chilean journalist, Delia Vergara, who had helped introduce her to the writings of some of the most influential American feminists of the time. With this exposure, plus conversations she had with Vergara, who was her age, Isabel Allende had found a new direction.

Vergara had an additional impact on Allende after her return to Chile. Vergara was planning to start a new magazine for Chilean feminists. She had read some of Allende's work and, as she put together a team of writers and journalists for the periodical, which included important Latin American feminists such as Malu Sierra and Amanda Paz, she contacted Isabel. She was especially interested in having Allende write a humor column. Through the first six months of 1967, Vergara prepared the format for the feminist publication. She launched the first issue in August 1967. The name of the new magazine for feminists was *Paula*.

At first, although Delia Vergara had contacted Allende about writing for *Paula*, Isabel was only a collaborator, not part of the magazine's permanent staff. Taking the opportunity to make a reputation for herself, Allende wrote her column with boldness and flair, emphasizing controversial subject matter. Initially, Allende wrote under a pseudonym—Francisca Roman—a combination of her mother's name and that of Tío Ramón. Allende's experiences with the magazine, as well as her other journalistic pursuits, helped her carve out a niche for herself in the world of journalism and also laid a foundation for her ventures into novel writing years later:

I was very serious about journalism, even though colleagues from that time believe that I invented my reports. I didn't invent them, I merely exaggerated slightly. The experience left me with several obsessions: I find I am forever on the prowl for news and stories, always with a pencil and notepad in my handbag for jotting down anything that catches my eye. What I learned then helps now in my writing: working under pressure, conducting an interview, doing research, using the language efficiently. I never forget that a book is not an end in itself. Just like a newspaper or a magazine, a book is a means of communication, which is why I try to grab the reader by the throat and not let go to the end.[84]

QUESTIONING EVERYTHING

Within the pages of *Paula*, Isabel Allende confronted many of the most controversial issues of the late 1960s. She "questioned everything that was institutionally sacred."[85] She was not afraid to write about politics, sex, marriage, social norms and values, and any other topic that aroused an emotional response from her readers. Her favorite topic was the struggle between the sexes, which she looked at from a feminist point of view. In part, Allende used the new publication to vent many of her feelings and frustrations about the patriarchy that was so entrenched in Chile. These weren't new feelings; the adult Isabel had experienced them for years. "My anger towards male authority and all types of authority continued even after my marriage. And it endures even today."[86]

In general, the new magazine was popular with younger readers, while the older, more conservative public was outraged. Splashed across its pages were articles and sidebars on everything considered taboo in Chilean society, including birth control methods, abortion, divorce, male chauvinism, political corruption, psychological disorders, drugs, and suicide. The idea of equality of the sexes—the mainframe concept around which *Paula* had been constructed—was unfathomable to many traditional-minded Chileans. As Allende explained in an interview: "It delved into politics, reported on radical movements around the world, and, in general, it touched on all that which had been untouchable up to then in Chile."[87]

Isabel Allende became comfortable in her new role as a journalistic provocateur. She was breaking all the rules of polite and restrained Chilean society and using her feminist views to mock nearly everything. As one writer has described her journalistic endeavors: "Seditious and iconoclastic, she set out to stir the hornet's nest of the sixties by ridiculing everyone."[88] Suddenly, Isabel Allende and her words had power.

While she worked for *Paula*, Allende was also involved with other journalistic projects. She wrote for the children's

ONE OF *PAULA'S* MOST CONTROVERSIAL VOICES

The launching of Chile's first feminist magazine, *Paula*, helped Isabel Allende find her journalistic voice. In one of the early issues, Allende described the various stages of the development of the male species from his origins as a caveman into the twentieth-century male. Among her examples was the man of the Roman Empire who "devoted himself to orgies and to killing Christians"* and the man of the Renaissance who "picked up his beloved's handkerchief but did not blow his nose in it."** Finally, she described the twentieth-century man: an insecure male living an unchallenging life, who "lives in cement mousetraps, eats canned fruit, buys on credit, plans his family, drives a van, and believes in statistics. He is born without pain, lives a life of boredom, and dies of cancer."***

In yet another tongue-in-cheek column, Allende wrote about husbands, placing them into various categories of archetypes, including "unfaithful husband, elegant husband, affectionate husband, henpecked husband, ideal husband, Latin husband, and vacation husband."† Of the Latin husband, Allende wrote: "Do not confuse the Latin husband with the Latin lover, his antithesis. These husbands vary according to whether they are magazine *Mampato* and also starred in her own television program, *Fijate que (Listen Up!)*.

Her voice cut across several layers of Chilean society. When she harshly poked fun at a particular theater play or television program, the public might stop watching it, leading to its cancellation. Looking back on her popularity during the late 1960s and early 1970s, Allende has her regrets: "To make a joke, I was capable of destroying someone. I wouldn't do that again, I will regret it for the rest of my life."[89]

All this writing in the name of feminism was essential to the woman Isabel Allende was becoming. She explains in her memoir, *Paula*: "My job on the magazine, and later in television, was

Mexican, Italian, Bolivian, Cuban, or Chilean. The common factor is that they covet their neighbor's wife."[††]

As she decried through her words the nature of some types of husbands, Allende wrote another piece for *Paula* that stirred up even greater controversy when she interviewed an important businesswoman who had been unfaithful to her husband. The result struck a strong chord with her readers as her "interview with the faithless wife . . . shattered the calm of Chilean society." [†††] The result was multilayered: Thousands of angry letters poured into the mailroom at the magazine, sales of the magazine doubled in a week, and Isabel was hired as part of the magazine's permanent staff.

 * Celia Correas Zapata, *Isabel Allende: Life and Spirits* (Houston, Tex.: Arte Publico Press, 2002), 37.
 ** Ibid.
 *** Ibid.
 † Ibid.
 †† Ibid., 37–38.
 ††† Isabel Allende, *Paula* (New York: HarperCollins Publishers, 1994), 143.

In the early 1970s, when this photograph was taken, Isabel Allende was making a name for herself as a controversial journalist. At the time, she was working as a columnist for *Paula* magazine and she hosted a comedy show and an interview program on a Santiago, Chile, television station.

an escape valve from the madness I inherited from my ancestors; without my work, the accumulated pressure would have landed me in a psychiatric ward. The prudish and moralistic atmosphere, the small-town mentality, and the rigidity of Chilean social norms at that time were overpowering."[90] For Allende, her feminist words were her way of fighting back and of getting out of the straitjacket of repression, both political and sexual.

Her husband, Michael, disliked many things about his wife's writing and expressive lifestyle. He did not like having a wife whose reputation as a writer was based on her support of feminism. He did not like the long skirts and "antique hats" she wore.[91] But he did not attempt to limit her voice. As Allende has asserted: "He forgave my extravagances because in real life I carried out my role as mother, wife, and housekeeper."[92] Allende's personal brand of feminism did not lead her to hate men. She loved her husband. Despite her "feminist diatribes," Isabel Allende "enjoyed the company of a man, her husband Miguel Frias, who loved her, respected her, and did not interfere in her work."[93] Allende's work on *Paula* lasted until 1974. By then, all of her coworkers on the magazine's staff had divorced. Allende was the only one whose marriage survived.

Turmoil in Chile

THE APPROACH OF FAME

With the arrival of the 1970s, Isabel Allende approached her thirtieth year. She had married a man she loved, was the mother of two children, and was becoming more famous with each passing year. Writing and appearing on a regular television program, she became a household name in many areas of Chile. She was developing a special brand of journalism, interviewing a wide variety of Chilean subjects, including "murderers, quasi-saints, prostitutes, and seers."[94]

Still, she sought additional outlets for her talents. She turned to writing plays, such as *The Ambassador* (1970), which was well received in Chilean theaters, and musical comedies, including *The Parvenu's Ballad* and *The Seven Mirrors*. Her life had become a sometimes precarious balancing act between home and work, personal and professional. But all this did not satisfy Allende. She was popular, especially with the younger Chilean audience, but she

It was the famous Chilean poet Pablo Neruda, pictured here, who suggested that Isabel Allende should become a novelist instead of a journalist. Allende took his advice to heart and has published 15 books, which have sold more than 35 million copies.

explained years later that "she did not consider that her work . . . as a journalist was exceptional."[95]

Despite her popularity, Allende had her critics. Some people did not appreciate her style of journalism. They thought she projected herself too much into her writing, which kept her from being objective. Delia Vergara, her editor at *Paula*, even accused her of "making up [her] interviews, without ever leaving the house, and of putting [her] own opinions in the mouths of [her] subjects."[96] Doubting her trustworthiness in reporting, Delia "rarely gave [Allende] important assignments."[97]

During an interview in 1972, Allende received the advice to abandon journalism completely. She was invited to visit the home of one of Chile's most famous poets, Pablo Neruda. Neruda was well-known among Chileans, had served at the Chilean Embassy in Paris, and was writing his memoirs at his coastal hacienda at Isla Negra. The poet was elderly and in poor health, so the opportunity to meet with him was a rare one. Allende prepared extensively for the interview. She bought a new tape recorder, read two biographies of the noted poet, and wrote a long list of questions to ask him. When she finally sat down with Neruda, he was warm and had kind things to say about her work in *Paula*. But he was concerned that she was not really cut out to be a journalist. He even told her: "My dear child, you must be the worst journalist in the country. You are incapable of being objective, you place yourself at the center of everything you do."[98] Then he made a suggestion that would have a lasting impact: "Why don't you write novels instead? In literature, those defects are virtues."[99] Little did Isabel Allende know at that moment that her life would change dramatically when, in just a few years, she decided to take the poet's advice and become a novelist.

POLITICAL UNREST

There would be other important changes for Isabel before she turned to writing fiction. She was not the only Allende who was in the public eye in the late 1960s and early 1970s. Her uncle Salvador (he was actually a cousin of Allende's father) was a public figure in his own right. He had helped establish the Chilean Socialist Party nearly 40 years earlier and served as the president of the national Senate from 1965 until 1969. During those years, he ran for the office of president of Chile three times and lost each time. Then, in 1970, he finally won the chief executive's office on his fourth attempt with only 38 percent of the vote. He had managed a win at the polls through the coop-eration of Chile's left-wing Unidad Popular ("Popular Unity") Party, which included members of the Communist Party.

During the campaign, alarmed that the Chilean left might gain power, the U.S. government became concerned that Communism might take further hold over Chile. The United States sent several million dollars to opposition parties and candidates in hopes that Salvador Allende would lose the election. But these opponents were divided among them-selves, which ensured his victory. Almost as quickly as Salvador Allende came to power, the U.S. president Richard Nixon and Secretary of State Henry Kissinger, began to con-sider ways to get him out of power. In the words of Kissinger: "There was no reason to watch as a country became commu-nist through the irresponsibility of its own people, and do nothing about it."[100] Nixon and Kissinger committed $10 million to the overthrow of Salvador Allende's Marxist-based government.

Through the early 1970s, Allende used his public office to try to bring about important changes in Chile. His goal was to establish true socialism through democratic means. He described his policy as "the Chilean road to socialism."[101] As the first Marxist president in Chilean history, Allende pushed the perennial Latin American policy of land reform and nationalized businesses and factories. He nationalized American-owned businesses, including International Telephone and Telegraph (ITT).

A NATION AT WAR

Unfortunately for Salvador Allende, he managed to antago-nize powerful groups in Chile, including the opposition party–controlled congress and judiciary. During his first three years as president, he also lost support from many Chileans, especially with his failed economic policies. The situation became even more difficult for the Chilean economy when the U.S. government decided to start an economic blockade of

Isabel Allende's uncle Salvador Allende (pictured here with Allende's mother) was elected president of Chile in 1970. Although he was responsible for making a number of reforms in education and health care, many people, especially in the United States, feared that he intended to make Chile a Communist country.

Chile. By the spring of 1973, "Chile was like a nation at war."[102] The country was on the brink of disaster. There were regular acts of political violence, including sabotage and terrorist threats at the hands of radical extremists from both ends of the political spectrum. Isabel Allende later described these difficult times:

Chile was living in a climate of insecurity and latent violence, and the heavy machinery of the government was grinding to a halt. . . . At night, [in] Santiago . . . the streets were dark and nearly empty. . . . Brigades of youthful Communists painted propagandistic murals on walls and bands of extreme rightists drove through the streets in automobiles with dark tinted-glass windows, firing blindly.[103]

President Allende spoke out against those who were intent on bringing down his government. He spoke until he "was hoarse from denouncing the sabotage, but no one listened to him, and he did not have enough people or sufficient power to deal with his enemies by force."[104]

As Isabel Allende witnessed these events that were bringing turmoil to her country, she remained concerned about what might happen next. Inflation reached crippling levels, soaring to 360 percent a year. There were constant food shortages. These became so alarming that "people spent hours waiting to buy a scrawny chicken or a cup of cooking oil, but those who could pay bought anything they wanted on the black market."[105] Among these people was Isabel Allende. She began "to hoard food obtained with the cunning of a smuggler."[106] She turned to black market sources to feed her family. Although she wanted to support her uncle and the work of the Popular Unity Party, things were getting worse with each passing month. In addition, further complicating events, the U.S. government's Central Intelligence Agency (CIA) was busy plotting the downfall of Salvador Allende.

The year 1973 would prove fateful for Chile, President Allende, and Isabel. Parliamentary elections held in March brought increased support to Popular Unity, but the party still did not represent a majority of Chilean voters. As for the military, the chief of the armed forces, General Carlos Prats, spoke out in favor of Chile's constitution, insisting that Salvador Allende be allowed to serve out his presidency without threat of intervention. But the right-wing factions did not intend to

In September 1973, the Chilean military overthrew the government, killing Salvador Allende. In this photograph, the presidential palace is under attack during the coup.

roll over and surrender power to Allende. In June, a military faction attempted an unsuccessful coup. Then, the Chilean Parliament declared Allende's government to be illegal, as well as the Popular Unity Party. Military officers began to call for change, even as General Prats stood firm. Soon, he was forced to resign, and Allende replaced him with General Augusto Pinochet, "an obscure career officer whom no one had ever heard of until then . . . and who swore to remain loyal to the democracy."[107] But Pinochet's promise of loyalty did not last long.

On September 11, 1973, Chile experienced the violence of a military coup against the Allende government. The military made its move with the encouragement of the CIA. It quickly developed into "the most violent military coup in twentieth-century South American history."[108] The presidential palace was bombed and Salvador Allende was killed. The military then dissolved the Chilean Congress and began a systematic campaign against groups of Allende supporters, including students, political leftists, and members of the urban working class. All this took place within the coup's first 24 hours. Pinochet, a former professor of geopolitics and student of the School of the Americas in Panama, quickly consolidated all government power in his own hands.

These events had a dramatic effect on the deposed president's relative, Isabel Allende. She later wrote about the significance of the coup and the complete alteration of her homeland's government and the death of her uncle:

> I suppose there are moments in all human lives in which our fate is changed or twisted and forced to follow a different course. That has happened several times in mine, but maybe one of the most defining was the military coup in 1973. Were it not for that event, it's clear that I would never have left Chile, that I wouldn't be a writer, and that I wouldn't be married to an American and living in California.[109]

But the coup had more of an impact than simply overthrowing Salvador Allende—it also helped to mold Isabel Allende, the famous writer. It became a line of demarcation for her: "I think I have divided my life [into] before and after that day."[110]

A COUP'S IMPACT

Although Isabel Allende was aware of the politics that led to the downfall of President Allende, in the days just before the military seized control of the government, she remained ever hopeful that violence might be avoided. She had continued her normal activities and routines up to the week of the coup. That week, she even had lunch with her uncle Salvador, "who had a 'beautiful dream' for Chile, and whom [I] deeply admired."[111]

That day, as they shared their meal, her uncle spoke enthusiastically about the future of their country. He told her that, if a serious challenge arose against his leadership, he would not leave the presidential palace "unless the people demanded it."[112]

When the coup did come, Isabel was shocked. As he had said he would, Salvador Allende remained in the presidential mansion to the very end, but his government collapsed, and he was assassinated. In later years, Isabel Allende wrote of taking refuge in a neighborhood school during the day of the coup,

SEPTEMBER 11: DAY OF THE COUP

By her own admission, nothing in Isabel Allende's life has had a greater impact on her than the military overthrow of her uncle, the president of Chile, Salvador Allende. Although the coup played itself out on a national stage, the day would prove extremely memorable to his niece, Isabel, then a young woman in her early thirties.

The coup began at dawn on September 11, 1973. The Chilean Navy mutinied first, and the example set by its rebellious sailors was soon followed by the army, then the air corps, and finally by the Chilean police force, the *carabineros*. President Allende heard of these events quickly that morning and immediately took refuge in the Palacio de la Moneda, where he was soon joined by a loyal band of "ministers, secretaries, staff, trusted doctors, some newspapermen, and friends"* who began building barricades of furniture against the palace's doors.

With the palace already under siege, surrounded by tanks and troops, President Allende remained resolute, telling his old political comrade: "I shall not resign, I shall leave La Moneda only when my term is ended, as president, or when the people demand it—or dead."** Even with these words, the military uncertain of her uncle's future, the future of Chile, or even her own personal future.

Her uncle was deposed and murdered, which dealt a serious emotional blow to Isabel. Her sadness was soon compounded by news of a second death, that of poet Pablo Neruda, which took place less than two weeks after the political uprising. Isabel Allende took to the streets of Santiago with other marchers and mourners who carried red carnations and joined the procession that followed Neruda's casket to its burial site. During the procession, shouts rose up on behalf of

began shelling the palace compound, bringing down "the thick, centuries-old walls and [setting] fire to furniture and drapes on the first floor."***

That afternoon, Isabel received a telephone call from a friend: Her uncle, President Salvador Allende, was dead. She called her parents in Buenos Aires to tell them of the tragic news, but they had already heard. Tío Ramón immediately resigned his post and lowered the flag at the embassy to half-mast. His resignation marked the end of nearly 40 years of service in the Chilean diplomatic corps. With the death of Uncle Salvador and the resignation of Tío Ramón, the Chilean military coup could not help but represent a personal loss for Isabel. The overthrow of her uncle's government represented a horrific turn of events. There were those in her country who "had succumbed to the insanity of violence."[†]

* Isabel Allende, *Paula* (New York: HarperCollins Publishers, 1994), 192.
** Ibid., 193.
*** Ibid.
† Ibid., 197.

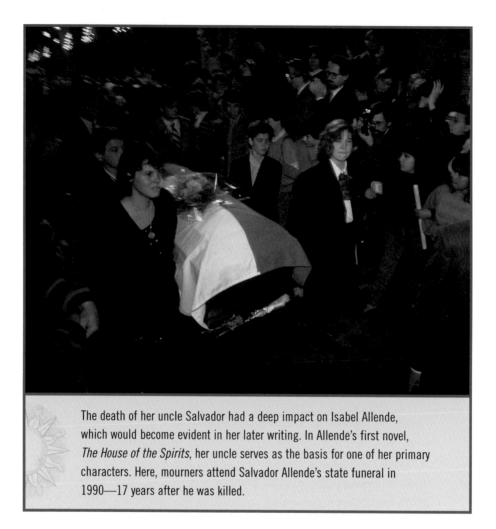

The death of her uncle Salvador had a deep impact on Isabel Allende, which would become evident in her later writing. In Allende's first novel, *The House of the Spirits*, her uncle serves as the basis for one of her primary characters. Here, mourners attend Salvador Allende's state funeral in 1990—17 years after he was killed.

both the dead poet and the assassinated president, Isabel's uncle: "Pablo Neruda! Present, now and forever! . . . Compañero Salvador Allende! . . . Present, now and forever!"[113]

Isabel Allende did not let these events destroy her. Within 48 hours of the fall of the Allende government, she was working with the Chilean underground, resisting the developing brutalities of the Pinochet regime in her own way. Through her contacts, she helped people who were being persecuted. She worked with churches to provide food and other necessities to oppressed families. She even convinced the president of her husband's company to donate money to the relief efforts. Using her old car, her "Citroen with [its] brightly painted flowers,"[114] she risked her own freedom to bring political refugees to safe houses.

Although her actions put her in danger, Allende would write in later years of the two-fold impetus for her efforts to challenge the Pinochet regime. Her work had a humanitarian element, motivated by a strong spirit of "compassion for such desperate people,"[115] but she also confessed that she was drawn to her efforts by "the irresistible attraction of adventure."[116] This desire to experience the thrill of secretly and defiantly opposing the military Chilean government goes to the heart of the kind of woman Isabel Allende is. In the best tradition of the brave and deeply emotional heroines who would later grace the pages of her novels, she came to "believe that life is a risky business requiring a daring and adventurous spirit and that individual actions can make a difference."[117] As a journalist, she took pains to record the stories of those who had been terrorized by the new regime. She spoke to the families of those who had been killed and wrote their stories of torture, terror, and death. She would one day weave some of these stories into her first novel, *The House of the Spirits*.

Exile and Redemption

AN OUTSPOKEN CRITIC OF THE GOVERNMENT

The aftermath of the military overthrow of President Allende had a ripple effect on both Chile in general and Isabel Allende. During the nearly 20 years that followed, terror, intimidation, and censorship ruled the lives of the people of Chile. With this new, conservative rule by force, Isabel Allende struggled to be a voice for her fellow Chileans. She wrote controversial, yet humorous, political pieces for the pages of *Paula*. More than six months after the coup, in April 1974, her column, titled "Pirates," appeared. The work was pointed and predictably insightful:

Pirates do not have to earn their living by the sweat of their brow; they earn it with other people's. They reach out a hand—the one holding a pistol—and appropriate their victims' earnings. When I was young I believed that pirates were people who stumped around with a wooden leg and a patch over one eye, but now I know some who wear suits by Juvens and shoes by Jarman. When they are satisfied with their accumulated treasures, they become politicians and settle down to govern . . . at least until something unexpected happens and they find themselves, as in Chile, frustrated in their wishes.[118]

She continued to write for *Paula* until she and her fellow staff members were fired and replaced by less controversial writers, who turned the outspoken, feminist publication into what Allende called "an exact replica of dozens of other frivolous publications for women."[119] After all, she noted, "in the eyes of the military, feminism was as subversive as Marxism."[120]

During the first year following the coup, circumstances in Chile got worse, especially for those opposed to the Pinochet regime. Even people who had fled Chile after the coup were not always safe. In 1974, the former head of the Chilean Army, General Prats, was assassinated while in exile in Argentina. Isabel's mother and Tio Ramón, fearing for their lives, went into hiding in Venezuela, a democratic Latin American country. Even as Allende continued her own resistance work against the military government, she became fearful enough to consider leaving Chile herself. As she later wrote: "I left because I could no longer stand the fear. I felt a visceral terror in Chile. It is difficult to talk about that. It is difficult to understand fear when you have not lived it. It is something that transforms us, that takes over completely."[121]

As her fear grew, Allende struggled with hives and had trouble sleeping. Then, in 1975, she received an anonymous death threat. Allende was forced to make a monumental decision. The pressure on her was growing intense. She decided to leave Chile for her own and her family's safety. Responding to the pressure placed on her by the new regime, as well as her growing personal fear, she packed up and left Chile for exile in Venezuela, with her husband, Michael, and their two children. As she later wrote, she spent her "first night in Caracas crying inconsolably in a borrowed bed."[122]

Augusto Pinochet ruled Chile as a military dictator from the time of the coup in 1973 until 1990, when the nation finally returned to a civilian government. Under his rule, political opponents were in constant danger of losing their freedom or even their lives.

The decision to abandon the struggle against the military control of her homeland was not an easy one, but it would prove more significant than Isabel Allende could have imagined at the time. Writing in later years, she analyzed the impact her self-imposed exile would have on her life:

It took me a year and a half to realize the risk I was running, and finally, in 1975, following a particularly agitated and danger-filled week, I left for Venezuela, carrying a handful of Chilean soil from my garden. A month later, my husband and my children joined me in Caracas. I suppose I suffer the affliction of many Chileans who left during that time: I feel guilty for having abandoned my country. I have asked myself a thousand times what would have happened had I stayed, like so many who fought the dictatorship from within, until it was overthrown in 1989. No one can answer that question, but of one thing I am sure: I would not be a writer had I not experienced that exile.[123]

A NEW LIFE AND HOME

Once Allende and her family left Chile and moved to Venezuela, they began a 13-year exile. For the family, and especially for Allende, the first of those years brought new challenges and personal difficulties from which her marriage to Michael never fully recovered. She had found professional fulfillment in her work as a journalist during those earlier years in Chile, writing for *Paula* and hosting her television program. She would find no such opportunities in Venezuela. There was no journalistic outlet there for her. Even her work for the Chilean underground was gone. Instead, her life became one of restlessness, anxiousness, and frustration. She did write some television scripts and did some work for the stage, but these were jobs that either paid poorly or not at all. Desperate for work, she took a job as a school administrator in Caracas. Although she had no head for figures, she was assigned to keep track of the school's financial accounts. For Allende, Venezuela came to represent a professional desert.

Allende and her family took up residence in a poor neighborhood, living "in an apartment in the noisiest and most densely populated district of the city."[124] She, Michael, and their children had been accustomed to living on two full-time incomes in Chile. Now they had to live on much less. They had to cut corners financially just to be able to afford to send Paula and Nicolás to school. The children were not happy and begged Allende almost every day to return to Chile.

Her mother and Tio Ramón lived in the same building as Allende's family, themselves exiles. Tio Ramón struggled with his own losses as a former Chilean diplomat. Allende later remembered how her stepfather "dressed every morning in one of his ambassador suits and went out to look for work, but . . . he never complained. His fall was more to be lamented than mine because he had risen higher, had lost more, was twenty-five years older, and must have had twice the dignity to be injured; even so, I never saw him depressed."[125] As for Allende, she often felt like a "prisoner in the apartment" but her family was safe "from the violence of the dictatorship, sheltered in the vastness of Venezuela."[126]

But life in Venezuela did have another impact on Isabel Allende, one that would forever change her life and its direction. While her home country of Chile had always been socially conservative, Venezuela gave Allende a sense of freedom she had not experienced before, even when she was writing feminist essays for *Paula*. She experienced "an intense assimilation of the sensuality and warmth of the Venezuelan people and landscape."[127] Allende was drawn into a world vastly different from that of Chile.

A STRAINED MARRIAGE

The change of scenery wasn't all good; it had devastating effects on her marriage. The restless Isabel Allende sought new sources of satisfaction to mask the dissatisfaction she was experiencing in her professional life. She and her husband were separated by his work. He had found an engineering job in the interior of Venezuela, working on a dam, leaving Allende behind in Caracas with the children. Looking back, she has come to believe that the "separation from my husband proved fatal . . . it marked the beginning of the end of our lives as man and wife."[128] Michael would return to Caracas on trips from the interior after spending weeks, even months, at his engineering job. Allende looked forward to his return each time, but knew they were drifting apart. "The man had just spent weeks in the jungle working to support his family . . . and I had no right to bother him with my heart's impatience,"[129] Allende would later write.

Unable to communicate and share their feelings, Isabel and Michael began living separate lives. Motivated by "unanswered desires and worries,"[130] she turned to other men, having several sexual affairs. Secretly, perhaps, Allende was looking for an excuse to end her marriage. She moved in and out of these relationships, finding only temporary fixes for the problems that plagued not only her marriage but her exiled life in a foreign land. She did not fall in love with any of the men in her life until she took up with a musician in 1978, an Argentine who had also left his own world of political turmoil for a life in Caracas. "He had escaped the death squads," Allende later wrote, "leaving a wife and two children behind . . . while he looked for a place to settle and find work, with a flute and a guitar as his only letter of introduction."[131] Allende met him while working on a musical. This time, the distraction was more than temporary. "He was as lonely and lost in Caracas as I, and I suppose that circumstance drew us together."[132] Allende was in love.

The affair only created more problems for Allende. Her relationship with Michael deteriorated further. Unable to concentrate on the normal events going on around her, she lost touch with her own children. They began to act out in their own ways. Her daughter, Paula, began throwing temper tantrums, slamming doors and crying in her room for hours with the door locked. Nicolás began to misbehave at school and his grades plummeted. Her mother and Tio Ramón, uncertain of the reason for Allende's odd behavior and her inability to keep her children's lives in order, questioned her and found out about her marital infidelities.

Then her lover gave Allende an ultimatum: Drop her life in Caracas and move with him to Spain, or their relationship would end. She refused to go, and he left without her. Instead, she went on a business trip with Michael to Paris. There, she thought about the direction her life was taking, and "while Michael was working I sat in the sidewalk cafes along the Champs-Elysees to think about the soap opera I was swallowed up in, tortured by the choice between memories of a flute on hot, rainy tropical afternoons and the natural pinpricks of guilt."[133] Meanwhile, her lover in Madrid tracked her down in Paris and continued to beg her to join him. Then, as Michael prepared to return to Caracas, Allende told him that she needed some time to herself. She did not return home, but instead boarded a train for Madrid.

After she spent two months with her lover, Michael, perhaps knowing more than he wanted to about his wife's errant behavior, came to Spain to find her. He knew about the affair, yet wanted to forgive her, to reclaim their lost relationship. "The past doesn't matter," he told Allende, "it will all work out, we will never mention this again."[134] Allende was certain that she wanted to revive her relationship with her husband. She was still in love with him, and although their marriage had, after 20 years, become less passionate, Michael was a good husband, a faithful man who had always given her stability and security. She said good-bye to her lover for the last time.

Allende had returned to the house of her family, but she was still unhappy. "When I definitively renounced my carnal passion for the indecisive Argentine musician," she later wrote, "there lay before my eyes a boundless desert of boredom and loneliness."[135] She still felt a keen sense of emotional separation from Michael. Their marriage did not end; it merely moved on as if nothing had ever happened.

Allende was still unable to find work as a journalist. She remained at her school job, just as unfulfilled and frustrated as ever. But the emotional events of that year had finally led her to understand that life was never going to be the way it had

While writing her first novel, Isabel Allende set a strict routine for herself, allowing for few interruptions. She kept up an exhausting pace, but the result—*The House of the Spirits*—was extraordinary.

been in Chile. The military was firmly in power, and there were no signs that it could be toppled. It was that year that Allende came face to face with reality: "In 1978, when total anguish had overwhelmed me, I decided to unpack my [emotional] bags, understand that I wasn't returning to Chile, and try to fit outside my country. It was my step from adolescence to adulthood."[136]

WRITING A LETTER

Over the next few years, Allende worked at her school administrator's job, finding little satisfaction in it. Then, in 1981, catastrophe struck, something that would change her life dramatically.

She received a phone call from a relative in Santiago telling her that her aged and beloved grandfather, Tata, was close to death. The old man was nearly 100 years old, having survived a stroke 20 years earlier. The news hit Allende hard and she wanted desperately to communicate with her grandfather one last time before he died. She made a momentous decision:

> Through the years, we had kept in touch by means of my steady stream of letters and his sporadic replies. I decided to write him

A CIRCLE OF FRIENDS

FELLOW WRITERS INSPIRE ISABEL ALLENDE

For more than a quarter century, Isabel Allende has produced an enviable body of fictional material, and her novels have brought her recognition both with the popular fiction-reading masses and the discerning world of academic writing. Her stories and their extraordinary qualities keep her readers coming back for more with the publication of each new book. Her fans remain extremely loyal, and Isabel continues to inspire their devotion through her ability to produce works that have a unique lyrical romanticism rooted in emotional honesty.

Unlike some writers, Isabel Allende has not made a constant or consistent practice of maintaining close friendships through the years with her fellow writers. Much of her time is devoted to her family, her writing, or her academic and speaking endeavors. However, throughout her career, writers have served to inspire her, whether they were exemplary journalists, novelists, essayists, or poets. She admits that such connections have given her incentive to become the writer she is today. Isabel specifically credits "all the great writers of the Latin American Boom."*

Allende, by her own admission, comes from the first generation of Latin American writers who were raised on the works of the previous generation of talented and creative Latin American writers. This earlier generation of Hispanic authors includes Gabriel García Márquez, Carlos Fuentes, Mario Vargas Llosa, Julio Cortazar, Jose Donoso, and others.

one last time, to tell him he could go in peace because I would never forget him and planned to bequeath his memory to my children and my children's children. To prove it, I began the letter with an anecdote about my great-aunt Rosa, my grandfather's first sweetheart. . . . From the first lines I wrote, other wills took control of my letter, leading me far away from the uncertain story of the family to explore the more secure world of fiction. During the journey, my motives became muddled, and the limits between truth and invention blurred.[137]

While each of these Latin American writers has served as inspiration to Isabel Allende, the literary technique they pioneered has helped shape her writing. That technique is called "magical realism."

The concept of magical realism was first identified as an artistic category by German art critic Franz Roh in the 1940s. However, the movement, which "is usually characterized by elements of the fantastic woven into the story with a deadpan sense of presentation,"** quickly spread into the realm of literature, where it was a major theme of García Márquez's and Argentinean Jorge Luis Borges's work.

In 1967, García Márquez published his great novel, *One Hundred Years of Solitude*, which used "magical realism" as an important part of its structure and thematic movement. (The novel became so successful that, by the end of the twentieth century, it had been translated into 30 languages and sold 10 million copies. García Márquez's novel established him as the leader of the Latin American literary movement that came to be called "The Boom."

It was García Márquez and his magical realism that has repeatedly inspired Isabel Allende's writing. She has repeatedly relied on its elements of transcending reality and its emphasis on spirituality and the spirit world in her novels. In a sense, the purveyors and creators of this movement have served as Isabel Allende's literary "Circle of Friends."

* Available online at *http://books.guardian.co.uk/authors/author/0, 5917,-3,00.html*
** Available online at *http://www.themodernword.com/gabo/gabo_mr.html*

Colombian writer Gabriel García Márquez was one of Isabel Allende's greatest literary influences. García Márquez was one of the first Latin American writers to employ magical realism—a literary style that blends elements of the real physical world with surreal occurrences and characters—in his books.

With inspiration coming through the windows from all directions, intent on telling the story of her family in her own way, in her own words, Isabel Allende was soon writing a novel. Just the week before, on New Year's Day, she had been bemoaning the approach of her fortieth birthday, feeling that she "had not until then done anything truly significant."[138]

Her wellspring of words and storytelling seemed to have no end. She was caught up in the telling of a family's tale, and, "as the characters came to life, they were more demanding than my own children."[139] As days of writing passed into weeks, Isabel Allende created a work schedule for herself, designed around her day job at school. She worked a double shift, putting in 12 hours from 7:00 A.M. until 7:00 P.M. Distracted by her ongoing efforts to write a lengthy work of fiction, Allende's work at the school became half-hearted: "I kept only half an eye on the accounts, the teachers, the students, and the classes, while all my real attention was centered on the canvas bag in which I carried the pages I churned out at night."[140]

No sooner would she reach home in the evening than she would eat supper with her family, shower, and sit down in front of a "small portable typewriter until fatigue forced me to bed."[141] The words seemed to come with tremendous ease, which Allende believed was the work of her grandmother, the clairvoyant, whispering words into her ear from the grave. After writing late into the night, she was up early the next morning and off to work. For months, her trance-like routine continued: "I wasn't sure what I was doing, because although my intention to write my grandfather a letter had quickly faded, I could not admit that I had launched into a novel, that idea seemed presumptuous."[142]

Although words were not new to Allende—she had, after all, spent two decades working as a journalist, playwright, scriptwriter, and essayist—they were taking a form she had never experimented with before. Allende continued writing her novel for a year until she realized she had a manuscript that was 500 pages long. She had never considered herself a *writer*; she was a *journalist*. But she had not been able to practice her skills for years. Her fiction work was taking form, taking on a life of its own. She was writing again, and, in doing so, she "felt that a long period of paralysis and muteness had ended."[143]

8

California Dreaming

A FIRST NOVEL

Driven by an exile bound by boredom and a frustrated need to write, Isabel Allende had spent an entire year writing her first novel. Its construction and development had preoccupied her nights and sent her into a self-imposed state of creativity. What had begun as a letter to her dying grandfather had become a 500-page family history filled with faces she had known in her life, as well as those she knew through a myriad of stories she had been told by generations of relatives who had lived before her and seen things she had not. Whether by design or by accident, the novel before her had taken on a certain life of its own. Uncertain what to do with the work she had created, Allende handed her "stack of stained, corrected pages to her mother to read."[144] Although her mother was initially shocked that Allende had created a novel by casting many of her family members as characters in her manuscript, she still told Allende to seek a publisher for her newly created work of fiction.

It would be the beginning of a new relationship between Isabel Allende and her mother, Francisca. Allende's mother became her daughter's editor and sent the manuscript off to various Latin American publishers in Argentina, Venezuela, and Chile. (Over the years since, Francisca has been the only person Allende will allow to correct her manuscripts.) There were many rejections until a Spanish literary agent, Carmen Balcells, took on the manuscript and managed to find a publisher. Balcells had a reputation as an agent to the best Latin American writers. In 1982, Isabel Allende's *The House of the Spirits* was published. The publisher flew Allende and Michael to Spain for the publication of the book. The night before they left for Europe, Allende's mother threw a massive family party. There, Tío Ramón handed her a mysterious package. As Allende unwrapped it, she found inside a copy of her book, which her stepfather "had obtained with the sleight of hand of a veteran dealmaker, importuning editors, mobilizing ambassadors on two continents, and utilizing the diplomatic pouch to get it to me in time."[145] The feeling she had at seeing her book for the first time was one she would never experience again in her life. Seeing the book's cover "with its rose-colored border and image of a woman with green hair, touched my deepest emotions."[146]

The publication of her first book started Allende on a lifelong adventure that has yet to come to an end. Indeed, her life would change in many ways during the decades that followed. *The House of the Spirits* proved to be a literary success. (However, since her novel cast the Pinochet regime in a negative light, her book was banned in her home country, Chile.) Hitting bookstores in the early 1980s, *The House of the Spirits* became part of the developing movement in literary circles to promote Latin American writers. Isabel's name—Allende—was one well known in and out of Latin America, so she already had a level of name recognition. But it would be her capacity and talent for storytelling and presenting significant themes that would make *The House of the Spirits* a best seller.

PROBLEMS AT HOME

As the success of writing and publishing her first best-selling novel became reality, she and Michael began to face serious problems that would alter the state of their lives and their marriage. The same week the novel was launched in Spain, Michael was facing the collapse of his business. A few years earlier, during the months after Allende's return from her affair with the musician, Michael had taken a serious gamble, starting his own construction company. Although business had been difficult at first, Michael's company had eventually landed a million-dollar contract, after he took on a partner from Venezuela. However, in the middle of Allende's trip to Spain, the bank that

FIRST NOVEL: *THE HOUSE OF THE SPIRITS*

The storyline of Isabel Allende's first novel, *The House of the Spirits*, reveals her ability to weave an extensive plot using a wide variety of interesting characters who are introduced through multiple generations of the same family. The novel's narrator, Alba, is a member of the fictionalized family, the Truebas. Alba is a granddaughter, born too late to have experienced all the family events found in the novel. She comes to know of events that precede her through the stories she is told orally and with the help of several journals kept by her grandmother. Once she arrives in the family, she is able to serve as an eyewitness to events that take place both within her life and that of her family.

There is, then, a shift in narrative style in Allende's book, as the narrator's sources change. In the first portion of the novel, Alba's narrative is driven by family tales and oral tradition that lend a mystical quality to the story. However, through the final third of the fiction narrative, she tells the tale with the nearly detached eye of a journalist, detailing the military coup perpetrated on the country's leader, who is also a member of the Trueba family.

was financing Michael's construction deal collapsed. His business took a serious hit, as his partner left with his investment money, "leaving Michael without work and up to his neck in a sinkhole of debts."[147]

The demise of Michael's business was followed by other problems for him and his family. He struggled with depression and began to have fainting spells. He was diagnosed with diabetes, but the fainting did not stop. It was not until a niece also became ill that doctors discovered the cause of Allende's husband's physical problems: Michael suffered from a rare metabolic disorder called porphyria. When they learned that the condition often ran in families, Isabel and Michael had their children tested. Unfortunately, they, too, tested positive for the illness.

All these problems soon had an effect on Michael's relationship with Isabel. In many ways, the couple had not fully recovered from Allende's earlier infidelities. These new challenges only made things worse between them, as Allende knew:

> By then, our marriage was like a glass bubble we were taking great precautions not to shatter; we treated each other with ceremonious courtesy and made obstinate efforts to stay together, despite the fact that every day our paths grew farther apart. We had respect and affection for one another, but the relationship weighed on me like lead; in my nightmares, I walked across a desert pulling a cart, and with every step my feet and the wheels sank into the sand. In that loveless period, I found escape in writing.[148]

A SECOND NOVEL

Allende's literary agent had told her that writing one novel did not make a person a writer "but that talent was proved with the second."[149] On the second anniversary of beginning the work that would become *The House of the Spirits*—January 8, 1983—Allende began to write her second work of fiction.

Once again, she worked by day at her school job, while spending her evenings writing in her kitchen.

As with her first fiction book, Allende chose a topic she felt passionately about. The novel was another work set in Chile with strong political overtones. She based the novel on events that the press had brought to light in the late 1970s: The uncovering of the massacre of 15 people by the Chilean military whose bodies had been discovered in some abandoned lime kilns.

The novel featured a military officer, Gustavo Morante, who refused to carry out orders to kill innocent civilians, only to face exile from his native homeland. In creating her novel, Allende "listened to the tapes [she had made during interviews] again, reread the press clippings, and called on my memory."[150] *Of Love and Shadows* was published in Spanish in 1984, and an English version was published three years later. Her second novel would be well received. With its publication, Allende decided to give up her day job and take up writing full-time.

With her second novel in print, Allende's world was changing dramatically. Tragedy struck her family with the death of Tío Ramón, the stepfather she had come to love dearly. Just months before his passing, he had announced to his family that he "wanted to go back to Chile to die,"[151] saying he was tired now that he was approaching 70. When he and Francisca left for their homeland, from which they had lived in exile for many years, Allende felt a terrible grief and sense of loss. Tío Ramón had long ago become, for her, "one of those loving and watchful patriarchs who gather all his loved ones beneath his protective cloak."[152]

ALTERED RELATIONSHIPS

Allende's life moved on. She continued to write and bought a large house in Venezuela after the publication of the English-version of *Of Love and Shadows* in 1987. Her husband, Michael, poured himself into remodeling the hacienda perched in the mountains, "making it into a sunny refuge with room to spare for visitors, relatives, and friends."[153] But, by then, the relationship between Isabel and Michael had "moved to an irreparable stage."[154] Allende experienced her final epiphany regarding her marriage during the summer of 1987:

> One of those warm June mornings in Caracas when storms gather early over the hills, Michael came down to my studio in the cellar to bring the mail. . . . I looked up and saw an unknown figure crossing the bare room, a tall, slim man with a gray beard and eyeglasses, bowed shoulders, and an opaque aura of fragility and melancholy. It was several seconds before I recognized my husband and realized what strangers we had become. I searched my memory for the embers of the carefree love of our twenties, but could not find even ashes, only the weight of dissatisfaction.[155]

Without hesitating, Allende announced that she wanted a separation; she and Michael mutually decided to bring their 25 years of marriage to an end. The annulment was finalized in 1987 with no rancor or bitterness. Both husband and wife knew they had grown too far apart to continue in their marriage. In the future, they would remain good friends.

After her marriage ended, Allende felt a new sense of loneliness and a strong need to get away. She was nearing her mid-forties, now without a husband in any sense of its meaning, and she wanted to "[run] away from explanations, and to outwit her sense of guilt."[156] Motivated by both personal and professional reasons, Isabel accepted that summer an invitation to deliver a series of worldwide lectures in the form of a book tour. Soon, she was traveling across continents, speaking to audiences as far away from her Latin American roots as Iceland. She spoke in at least a dozen North American cities, including San Francisco, the last leg of her two-month tour. There, she met an American admirer, a local lawyer named

Isabel Allende met Willie Gordon in San Francisco while she was on a book tour promoting one of her novels. They married in 1988, and Allende moved to California to be with her new husband.

Willie Gordon. He had read *Of Love and Shadows* and "had suffered for the characters and thought that in that book he had found the kind of love he wished for but had never experienced."[157] (He had received the book as a 50th birthday present.) A female professor introduced Gordon to Allende, referring to him as "the last heterosexual bachelor in San Francisco."[158] Before the evening was over, Allende felt a strong attraction:

> I dined with a group around a table in an Italian restaurant; Willie sat facing me, with a glass of white wine in his hand, saying nothing. I admit that I felt a certain curiosity about this Irish-looking North American lawyer with an aristocratic appearance and silk tie who spoke Spanish like a

Mexican *bandido* and had a tattoo on his left hand. There was a full moon, and the velvety voice of Frank Sinatra was crooning "Strangers in the Night" as our ravioli was served. This is the kind of detail that is forbidden in literature; in a book, no one would dare combine a full moon with Frank Sinatra.[159]

That evening, Allende asked Gordon to tell her his life story. As he did so, she discovered, to her surprise, that she "had stumbled upon one of those rare gems treasured by storytellers: this man's life was a novel."[160] That night, Allende could not sleep. The following morning, Willie Gordon tracked her down, inviting her to his home for dinner. Although she imagined a romantic evening in the lawyer's secluded California hillside estate, she found his home cluttered and chaotic, filled with a half dozen young people, including two sons and a stepson from his previous marriage. It was September, but Allende saw Christmas ornaments still hanging in a corner of the dining room, "with ten months accumulation of cobwebs."[161] The house was a confused scene of undisciplined children, both hyperactive and drugged-out; there were dead fish in the aquarium and a howling dog, but she and Willie escaped to his bedroom. She said, "To me, Willie represented a new destiny in another language and a different country; it was like being born again, I could invent a fresh version of myself only for this man."[162]

The next day, Allende flew back south to Caracas. She wasted no time putting together a mock "contract" for Willie to sign, an invitation for the two of them to commit themselves to a permanent relationship. When Willie signed the document and returned it, she packed her bags once more and took a flight to California, which remains her home today. Allende and Gordon were married on July 17, 1988. She once stated in an interview that Willie Gordon was first drawn to her through her second novel, *Of Love and Shadows*: "I am convinced that he married the book, not me."[163]

LIVING IN THE UNITED STATES

At first, Allende's transition to a new husband and a permanent move to the United States caused some big changes in her life. She was not comfortable speaking English and had always considered the United States a bullying empire. Then, there were Gordon's children. Although her own son and daughter—Paula and Nicolás—had experienced their own personal problems over the years, they were no match for the excesses of Willie's sons and daughter. There was a hyperactive 10-year-old, an older son who took drugs, and a daughter who had turned to prostitution to pay for her heroin habit. Allende returned to her domestic side and took well-intended steps to establish some sort of consistency and order within the Gordon house. During this period of extreme changes, she could not find enough time to write another novel, though she had already penned her third novel, *Eva Luna*, which was published in Spain in September 1987, just before she met Gordon. Instead, she turned to short stories and wrote whenever she could. The result was *The Stories of Eva Luna*, which was published in 1989.

As a South American taking up residence in North America, Allende struggled with situations she had not faced before in Chile or Venezuela. In a 1988 interview, she observed three significant changes in her daily life brought about by her move to the United States: taking up the role as domestic housewife "without the benefit of the inexpensive live-in household help"[164] she had been accustomed to in Latin America; the media saturation she experienced as a successful novelist; and working in two languages, Spanish and English. (Over the years, Allende's English-speaking skills improved significantly. Today, when she lectures, even to Hispanic audiences, she speaks in English, rather than have her Spanish translated by an interpreter.) Life in the United States afforded other opportunities for Allende who, by then an established novelist, was invited to teach writing. In 1988 and 1989, she taught classes at Barnard College, the University of Virginia, and the University of California, Berkeley.

A RETURN HOME

Even as Allende was adapting to a new life in a new country, events in Chile were bringing about important political changes. For 15 years, General Pinochet had ruled with a strong hand, not allowing political opposition and carrying out violence against anyone who defied his power. But now, Pinochet had managed to maneuver himself into a difficult corner. To legitimize his rule, he had authorized a clause in the Chilean constitution that called for a popular vote in 1988 to make him president. Should his government fail to win the support of the people's vote, Pinochet promised to call for democratic elections in 1989. Although Pinochet tried to limit opposition in the vote, the Chilean people were tired of his oppressive rule and voted him and his government out of office. The aging general had no choice but to abide by his promise to allow free elections. In the spirit of this new openness, Allende boarded a plane with Gordon by her side and returned to her homeland, setting foot on Chile's soil for the first time in 13 years. She had left as a frightened journalist and was returning as a successful novelist. At the airport, she was greeted by fans. It was a sublime moment for her:

> I cannot describe the emotion I felt when we crossed the majestic peaks of the cordillera of the Andes and I stepped onto the soil of my homeland, breathed the warm valley air, heard the accent of our Spanish . . . I was so weak in the knees, I had to lean on Willie as we passed through customs. . . . That return is the perfect metaphor for my life. I had fled from my country, frightened and alone, one wintry, cloudy late afternoon, and returned, triumphant, on my husband's arm one splendid summer morning. My life is one of contrasts, I have learned to see both sides of the coin. At moments of greatest success, I do not lose sight of the pain awaiting me down the road, and when I am sunk in despair, I wait for the sun I know will rise farther along.[165]

Among the people she visited in Chile were her mother and Michael, who had remarried. She and Michael "walked through the streets of our old neighborhood and rang the bell of the house where Paula and Nicolas grew up."[166] They were invited in by strangers, and allowed to take a sentimental journey through each room. Then, she said good-bye to her old lover and friend.

REACHING BEYOND HER CHILEAN ROOTS

Today, Isabel Allende is recognized as one of the most important Hispanic writers and novelists in the world. Over the past 30 years, she has been a journalist, editor, essayist, columnist, autobiographer, and novelist.

Until the 1960s, only Spanish-speaking audiences read the works of Latin American or Hispanic writers. Few of their works were translated into other languages, especially English. Those novelists who did break the accepted mold included the Mexican writer Carlos Fuentes and Mario Vargas Llosa of Peru. Then, in 1967, a Colombian fiction writer named Gabriel García Márquez published *One Hundred Years of Solitude*. The successful novel was translated into English and found a worldwide audience. García Márquez's work marked the beginning of a sea change in Hispanic literature still referred to as *el Boom*, or "The Boom." The translation of Spanish literature into other languages signaled the international acceptance of Hispanic writers by non-Spanish readers.

At the center of this "Boom" literature was a writing technique called magical realism. It is a literary style that blends elements of the real physical world with surreal occurrences and characters. In such novels, characters can predict the future, defy the laws of physics, or simply do things outside the limitations of the real world. Magical realism became a recurring element used by many Latin American writers.

But these writers were all men. It was Isabel Allende who blazed the feminist trail and became one of the first important Hispanic female

The following year, Allende returned again to Chile and voted in her country's first national election since 1970. Pinochet was voted out, and the first legitimate president since her uncle, Salvador Allende, was elected.

writers. She, too, employed the element of magical realism, but Allende's role as a Latin American writer has gone beyond her deft use of this unique literary style. Her contribution to the scope and popularity of modern Latin American literature is undeniable. In 1991, the writer Fernando Alegria noted the impact Allende was having on literature in her native country: "In my recent trip to Chile I had the sensation that Isabel Allende was present everywhere: her books are in all the book stores, people read them and talk about them. . . . At the Conference on Women Writers that took place in Santiago, her name was mentioned many times, her books discussed."[*]

But Alegria also understood that there was another phenomenon occurring in Latin American literature at that moment. He was aware of a "new narrative voice" that existed among the short stories and novels by Latin American writers, "and that is the voice of women."[**] Allende, however, believes that her literary contributions are more significant. She does not immediately or exclusively identify herself as a female author or as a *Chilean* author. In an interview, she expressed her view: "I find it very difficult to see myself as a Chilean writer. . . . I feel more and more Latin American. I talk a lot about being Latin American. This, I feel, is a new phenomenon in the continent."[***]

[*] John Rodden, ed. *Conversations with Isabel Allende* (Austin: University of Texas Press, 1999), 201.
[**] Ibid.
[***] Ibid., 202.

The
Infinite
Plan

AN EXTREME LOSS

With the arrival of the 1990s, Isabel Allende set out to write her fourth novel, using a protagonist based on her second husband, Willie Gordon. The new novel, *The Infinite Plan*, was set against the backdrop of California and her main character was a lawyer. She managed to complete the work by 1991. That December, while in Madrid attending a book publication party for *The Infinite Plan*, Allende received devastating news. Her daughter, Paula, was extremely ill with porphyria, the metabolic disorder that her father, Michael, was diagnosed with a few years earlier. Allende arrived at her daughter's bedside in time to speak to her. Crying, she told her ill adult child that she loved her. Paula replied: "I love you, too, Mama."[167] These would be her final words to her mother. Delirium set in and, within a couple of days, Paula slipped into a coma and never spoke again.

Her daughter's illness marked the beginning of a long nightmare for Isabel Allende. As Paula's coma stretched on for weeks and

Isabel Allende's daughter, Paula, died in 1992, after a long battle with porphyria, an often-fatal metabolic disorder. In 1996, in honor of her daughter, Allende established the Isabel Allende Foundation, which supports organizations that help women and children in need.

then months, Allende stayed in Madrid, unable to leave her daughter. She rented a small apartment and went to sit at Paula's bedside every day, along with Paula's grandmother, Francisca. When it appeared that Paula was not going to come out of the coma, Allende arranged for her to be flown to San Rafael, California, where she and Willie lived. It was there that Paula died on December 8, 1992, one year to the day after she had fallen into a coma.

Through the yearlong ordeal, Allende struggled with her feelings and with doubts that she would ever be able to write again if her daughter did not recover. To help her handle her struggle and pain, her literary agent suggested that Allende write down her thoughts. Allende directed her writing to her seriously ill daughter. With Paula's death, Allende began writing a new manuscript on January 8, 1993. Her new work had a dual purpose. (Throughout her career as a fiction writer, Isabel Allende has started writing each of her books on January 8.) In this new book, she wrote her memoirs and alternated those pages of her past against the events she experienced as Paula lay in her coma. In part, she wrote these pages for her daughter, stating in her opening sentence: "Listen, Paula, I am going to tell you a story, so that when you wake up you will not feel so lost."[168] Penning this work proved to be a form of therapy for Allende. The result was a book aptly titled *Paula*, which was published in 1994. Other than her first novel, *The House of the Spirits*, this work, so personal, yet cathartic, would become one of Isabel Allende's most popular.

A SUCCESSFUL CAREER

The 1990s were a period of solidification in Isabel Allende's literary career. Some of her earlier novels were made into motion pictures. In 1993, a film based on *The House of the Spirits* was released, directed by Billie August, and starring Glenn Close, Jeremy Irons, Meryl Streep, Antonio Banderas, and Winona Ryder. In 1995, the British Broadcasting Company (BBC) presented a documentary titled *Listen Paula*, based on Allende's book. But even as book-to-movie deals became common for Allende, she still found herself facing one of a writer's worst fears. Toward the mid-1990s, still struggling with the grief of losing her only daughter, Allende continued to suffer from depression that seemed to lead to a serious case of writer's block. She began to doubt her capacity to continue as a novelist and worried that she might have created her last fictional

Although Isabel Allende was distraught over the death of her daughter, she continued to write. In fact, one of her most noteworthy books, *Paula*, published in 1994, was written as a tribute to her daughter.

characters. In an interview in 1995, she expressed concern that she might never write again.

She was, in fact, at a reflective stage in her writing. She had already written six books in 12 years: *The House of the Spirits, Of Love and Shadows, Eva Luna, The Stories of Eva Luna, The Infinite Plan,* and *Paula.* Perhaps, she thought, she had written all that she had hidden within herself. But rather than turn away from writing altogether, she moved away, briefly, from her fiction, choosing to create a whimsical yet sensuous new work that combined sex and food, a pastiche of cooking recipes and love potions and aphrodisiacal concoctions. Representing a type of recipe book for lovers, her book was titled *Aphrodite: A Memoir of the Senses.* For Isabel Allende, the book was a tonic, a wake-up call to take up residence in the real world once more. While on a book tour in 1998 for *Aphrodite*, Allende seemed to have finally recovered from the loss of her daughter, Paula, as much as a mother ever could. She claimed in one of her many interviews that putting together her unique book of love recipes had "helped her rediscover a capacity to live in the present."[169] Her writer's block was gone.

In the years that followed, Isabel Allende added to her fiction list. She returned to novel writing with the publication of two

BEING HISPANIC

THE FOCUS OF ISABEL ALLENDE'S NOVELS

Isabel Allende's novels are popular throughout the world, from Europe to North America to Asia. Her audiences cross ethnic, racial, and national lines. Her works are translated into dozens of languages. Her eclectic global audience continues to support her work, whose themes are universal, yet are transmitted, typically, through Latin American characters, especially strong Hispanic women. However, despite being a proud Latin American writer, Allende lives in the United States.

But this self-imposed exile from her Latin American origins has not drawn Allende away from her Hispanic heritage, one that was influenced by living in more than one Latin American country. She was born in Lima, Peru, of Chilean parents and raised in both Latin American countries at various times. As an adult, she lived in Bolivia, Chile, and later Venezuela, from where she went into exile in 1975. Today, Allende lives in San Rafael, California, which helps keep her in close and constant contact with Hispanic culture. Although she has stated, "I can live and write anywhere,"* Allende has remained quintessentially Hispanic. Despite her self-assuredness about her writing environment, she will always remain a writer who is influenced by her heritage.

works in rapid succession: *Daughter of Fortune* (1999), richly set in the nineteenth century between Chile and California, and *Portrait in Sepia* (2000), its sequel. The two books serve as the second and third entries in a loosely connected trilogy that began with *The House of the Spirits*. As Allende approached the end of her second decade as a novelist, her works were as popular as ever. During one nine-day period in January 2000, her novel *Daughter of Fortune* sold 350,000 copies in Italy alone.

In more recent years, she has written three fiction books for young adults: *The City of the Beasts* (2002), *Kingdom of*

She is today working at the epicenter of Latin American literature. It was her Hispanic legacy that inspired her to pen the words of her first novel, *The House of the Spirits*, back in 1982. As with many writers of fiction, Allende took from her childhood experiences and memories and spun her first novel using her Latin American roots as her springboard. Many of her characters were drawn from life, including relatives, such as her mother and grandmother. The result was a first novel that would set the standard for her future works. Two later novels—*Daughter of Fortune* (1999) and *Portrait in Sepia* (2000)—would follow successive generations of the same Latin American family that she had introduced in *The House of the Spirits*.

As in nearly all of her novels, Allende has remained true to her strong Hispanic female characters. It has been a goal that she has kept from the beginning. She has used her literary skills to create Hispanic heroines who reveal to her readers the disadvantages women in Latin America have always faced. This goal has set her apart from many other writers. While illustrating to her readers—especially her myriad of female devotees—that Latin American women may not only survive against the oppressions and injustices placed upon them by Hispanic cultural norms and practices, she also makes it clear that Hispanic women can, individually and collectively, change their future.

* Isabel Allende, *My Invented Country, A Memoir* (New York: Perennial, 2004), 197.

Isabel Allende's book *Daughter of Fortune* was published in 1999 and immediately garnered praise. The historical novel, set in nineteenth-century Chile and California, recounts the tale of Eliza Sommers, who travels to the United States during the gold rush of 1849.

the Golden Dragon (2003), and *Forest of the Pygmies* (2005). This exciting trilogy of books has introduced younger readers to the exploits of the teenage adventurer Alexander Cold, who is whisked around the world—from the rain forests of the Amazon to the forbidding Himalayas to the savannahs of Africa—in the company of his indomitable grandmother Kate. The works represent a departure from Allende's adult themes, but have returned her to writing for children, which she did in the early 1970s.

In the spring of 2005, *Zorro: A Novel* was published. Keying off the popular fiction hero whose exploits are set in the Spanish California of the late 1700s, Allende imagined the masked adventurer's early years and the circumstances and motivations that led him to become a champion of the poor and the exploited. (In Allende's version, young Zorro is the son of a Spanish don and a female Shoshone fighter.) The result is a colorful, swashbuckling work of fiction with its roots lying in Allende's own past, when she was still living in Chile under the military rule of General Pinochet, helping those suffering under his regime.

A NOVELIST FOR TODAY

Today, Isabel Allende continues to write fiction as she has done for the past 25 years. There are plans to adapt several of her novels into motion pictures. Others have been turned into other art forms, including operas and ballets. Her books have been translated into more than two dozen languages and have been best sellers in Latin America, the United States, Europe, and Australia. In all, Isabel Allende's books have amassed sales of more than 35 million copies. She has received dozens of honors and awards for her writing, as well as several honorary doctorates from leading universities and colleges, including New York State University, Columbia College, and Illinois Wesleyan. Both Allende and her works have been honored as annual "Best Novels" and "Author of the Year" in Germany, Portugal, Switzerland, Mexico, and her native Chile. In 2004, she was inducted into the American Academy of Arts and Letters, a singular honor for a writer.

Isabel Allende's popularity defies borders. As one writer has explained in describing Allende's international appeal:

> If you go to Mexico and walk through the streets there, you will see the covers of Isabel's books on Insurgentes Avenue; if you go to Buenos Aires, you will see them in the bookstores on Calle Florida; if you find yourself in Madrid, they're on the Gran Via; in France, Italy, Germany, and Portugal, Isabel Allende's books are prominently displayed. The jackets vary by edition and language, some done by great artists and others by unknown artists.[170]

Although she continues to live in California, she still holds her homeland, Chile, close to her heart. She returns once or twice a year to keep up with life along the Cordilleran chain of the Andes to visit friends and relatives, and to maintain that connection between the Isabel Allende of the past and the Isabel Allende of the present. She has explained the nature of her split world in her own words: "For the moment California is my home and Chile is the land of my nostalgia. My heart isn't divided, it has merely grown larger. I can live and write anywhere."[171]

Isabel Allende's world remains one of accessibility. She continues to pour herself into each new novel, revealing characters that are as rich and compelling as the character she has created in herself. Her books allow her to speak her mind and to tell her own story and the stories of others. In one of her recent books, *My Invented Country*, a short memoir in which she places herself and her native homeland of Chile side by side, she summarizes the impact becoming a writer and novelist has had on her life:

> Don't believe everything I say: I tend to exaggerate. . . . Let's just say, to be completely honest, that I can't be objective, period. In any case, what's most important doesn't appear in my biography or my books, it happens in a nearly imperceptible way in the secret chambers of the heart. I am a writer because I was born with a good ear for stories, and I was lucky enough to have an eccentric family and the destiny of a wanderer. The profession of literature has defined me. Word by word I have created the person I am and the invented country in which I live.[172]

Chronology and Timeline

1942   Isabel Allende is born in Lima, Peru, to Tomás Allende, a Chilean diplomat, and Francisca Llona Barros.

1945   Isabel's parents have their marriage annulled; her mother returns to Chile with the children to live with Isabel's grandfather.

1953–58   Francisca marries Ramón Huidobro, another Chilean diplomat; "Tio" Ramón moves the family first to Bolivia, then to Beirut, where Isabel attends a private English school.

1958   With the outbreak of unrest in Lebanon, Tio Ramón and Francisca send Isabel to Chile to live with her grandfather; there, she attends secondary school and meets Michael Frias, an engineering student, who will become her husband.

1959–65   Following her graduation from secondary school, Isabel takes a job with the United Nations FAO (Food and Agriculture Organization).

1962   Isabel and Michael Frias are married.

1963   Isabel gives birth to her first child, a daughter named Paula.

1964–65   Isabel and Michael tour Europe along with their daughter, visiting Belgium and Switzerland.

1966   The family returns to Chile, where Isabel gives birth to her second child, a son named Nicolás.

1967–74   Isabel begins her work as a journalist, taking a job writing a feminist column for *Paula* magazine.

1970–75   Isabel becomes a pioneer in broadcast journalism, working for a television station in Santiago and hosting two programs, a comedy show and an interview program.

1973   The president of Chile, Salvador Allende, Isabel's uncle, is murdered during a military coup; Augusto Pinochet takes control of the country.

1973–74 Isabel writes for a children's magazine, *Mampato*, and writes a pair of children's stories.

1973–75 While continuing her work as a journalist, Isabel works secretly helping those politically oppressed by the Pinochet regime.

1975 As political pressure on Isabel mounts, she and her family leave Chile and move to Venezuela, where they remain in exile for the next 13 years; the next few years are difficult for Isabel, both professionally and personally—she takes an unfulfilling job with a Caracas newspaper, *El Nacional*.

1978 Isabel and Michael separate and she spends two months in Spain; eventually, she returns home to Michael.

1979–82 Isabel takes another unfulfilling job, this time as an administrator at a Caracas secondary school.

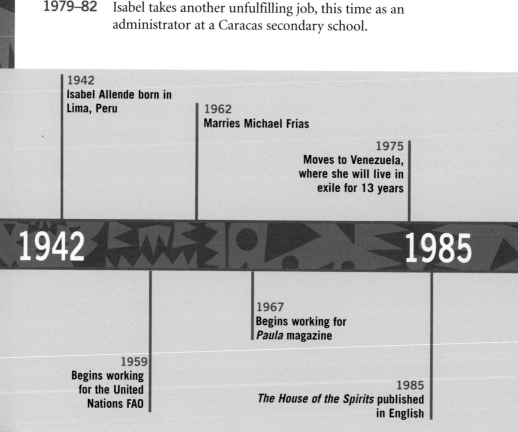

1942
Isabel Allende born in
Lima, Peru

1962
Marries Michael Frias

1975
Moves to Venezuela,
where she will live in
exile for 13 years

1942

1985

1967
Begins working for
Paula magazine

1959
Begins working
for the United
Nations FAO

1985
The House of the Spirits published
in English

1981 When Isabel receives word that her grandfather is dying back in Chile, she begins writing a letter to him that becomes her first novel.

1982 Isabel's first novel, *The House of the Spirits*, is published in Spain and banned in Chile; it is the beginning of her new career as a fiction writer.

1984 Isabel's second novel, *Of Love and Shadows*, is published.

1985 *The House of the Spirits* is published in English, with great success; Isabel is invited to teach in the United States.

1987 Isabel and Michael's marriage is annulled; her third novel, *Eva Luna*, is published in Spain; during a book tour in California, Isabel meets William Gordon, a San Francisco lawyer and Isabel moves to California; *Of Love and Shadows* is published in English.

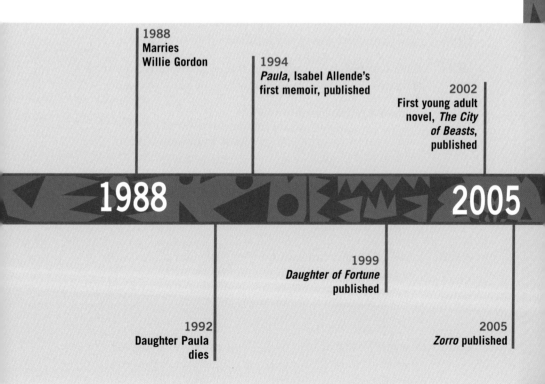

1988
**Marries
Willie Gordon**

1994
***Paula*, Isabel Allende's
first memoir, published**

2002
**First young adult
novel, *The City
of Beasts*,
published**

1988

2005

1999
***Daughter of Fortune*
published**

1992
**Daughter Paula
dies**

2005
***Zorro* published**

1988	Isabel and Willie Gordon are married; *Eva Luna* is published in English.
1989	*The Stories of Eva Luna* is published in Spain; Isabel becomes a guest writer for the University of California, Berkeley.
1990	With the military regime voted out and democracy restored in Chile, Isabel returns to her home country, where she receives a literary prize from the newly elected president.
1991	*The Stories of Eva Luna* is published in English; later that year, Isabel's daughter, Paula, slips into a coma from an inherited condition.
1992	After a year in a coma, Paula dies.
1993	Isabel's novel *The Infinite Plan* is published by HarperCollins in English; a film version of *The House of the Spirits* is released.
1994	Isabel's memoir *Paula* is published.
1997	After a few years of grieving, Isabel's *Aphrodite* is published in Spain.
1998	*Aphrodite* is published in English.
1999	Isabel's novel *Daughter of Fortune* is published both in Spanish and English.
2000	Isabel's next novel, *Portrait in Sepia*, is published in Spain.
2002	Isabel's young adult novel *The City of Beasts* is published in Spanish and English.
2003	Isabel's second young adult novel, *Kingdom of the Golden Dragon*, is published.
2004	Isabel is inducted into the American Academy of Arts and Letters.
2005	The third book of her young adult trilogy, *Forest of the Pygmies*, is published; her latest adult novel, *Zorro*, also is published.

Notes

Chapter 2

1 Isabel Allende, *My Invented Country, A Memoir* (New York: Perennial, 2004), 28.

2 John Rodden, ed., *Conversations with Isabel Allende* (Austin: University of Texas Press, 1999), 71.

3 Ibid.

4 Isabel Allende, *Paula* (New York: HarperCollins Publishers, 1994), 14.

5 Celia Correas Zapata, *Isabel Allende: Life and Spirits* (Houston, Tex.: Arte Publico Press, 2002), 15.

6 Ibid.

7 Allende, *Paula*, 13.

8 Rodden, 71.

9 Allende, *My Invented Country*, 28.

10 Zapata, 2.

11 Ibid., 3.

12 Allende, *My Invented Country*, 29.

13 Allende, *Paula*, 17.

14 Ibid., 18.

15 Allende, *My Invented Country*, 29.

16 Ibid., 32.

17 Ibid.

18 Rodden, 169.

19 Quoted in Allende, *My Invented Country*, 70.

20 Ibid., 72.

21 Rodden, 72.

22 Allende, *Paula*, p. 51.

23 Rodden, 72.

24 Ibid.

25 Ibid.

26 Ibid.

Chapter 3

27 Allende, *My Invented Country*, 73.

28 Allende, *Paula*, 23.

29 Allende, *My Invented Country*, 107.

30 Zapata, 8.

31 Rodden, 168.

32 Allende, *Paula*, 53.

33 Rodden, 168.

34 Allende, *Paula*, 59.

35 Ibid.

36 Zapata, 26.

37 Allende, *Paula*, 59.

38 Ibid., 60.

39 Ibid.

40 Ibid.

41 Zapata, 26.

42 Allende, *Paula*, 62.

43 Zapata, 26.

44 Allende, *Paula*, 64.

45 Ibid.

46 Ibid., 65.

47 Ibid.

48 Zapata, 27.

49 Allende, *Paula*, 71.

Chapter 4

50 Ibid., 88.

51 Ibid.

52 Allende, *My Invented Country*, 111.

53 Ibid.

54 Ibid.

55 Allende, *Paula*, 88.

56 Ibid., 89.

57 Ibid., 90.

58 Ibid.

59 Ibid., 91.

60 Quoted in Allende, *Invented Country*, 113.

61 Quoted in Allende, *Paula*, 95.

62 Ibid.

63 Ibid., 96.

64 Ibid.

65 Ibid., 97.

66 Ibid., 98.

67 Allende, *My Invented Country*, 122.

68 Rodden, 173.

69 Allende, *Paula*, 113.

70 Ibid.

71 Ibid., 114.

Chapter 5

72 Allende, *My Invented Country*, 125.
73 Ibid., 124.
74 Ibid.
75 Allende, *Paula*, 135.
76 Ibid., 134.
77 Ibid.
78 Ibid., 135.
79 Ibid., 135–136.
80 Ibid., 136.
81 Ibid., 137.
82 Ibid., 138.
83 Ibid.
84 Allende, *My Invented Country*, 127–128.
85 Zapata, 37.
86 Rodden, 175.
87 Ibid., 177.
88 Zapata, 38.
89 Ibid.
90 Allende, *Paula*, 145.
91 Ibid.
92 Ibid.
93 Zapata, 38.

Chapter 6

94 Linda Gould Levine, *Isabel Allende* (New York: Twayne Publishers, 2002), 5.
95 Zapata, 51.
96 Allende, *Paula*, 172.
97 Ibid.
98 Ibid., 182.
99 Ibid.
100 Allende, *My Invented Country*, 149.
101 Available online at *http://www.encyclopedia.com/html/A/AllendeIS.asp*.
102 Allende, *Paula*, 183.
103 Ibid., 184.
104 Ibid., 185.
105 Allende, *My Invented Country*, 152.
106 Allende, *Paula*, 185.
107 Ibid., 186.

108 Thomas Skidmore and Peter Smith, "Chile, Democracy, Socialism, and Repression," *Modern Latin America*, ed. Thomas Skidmore and Peter Smith (New York: Oxford University Press, 1984), 141.
109 Allende, *My Invented Country*, 141–142.
110 Levine, 7.
111 Ibid.
112 Ibid.
113 Allende, *Paula*, 214.
114 Levine, 8.
115 Ibid., 9.
116 Allende, *Paula*, 218.
117 Levine, 9.

Chapter 7

118 Zapata, 40.
119 Allende, *Paula*, 201.
120 Ibid.
121 Levine, 8.
122 Allende, *My Invented Country*, 164.
123 Ibid.
124 Allende, *Paula*, 243.
125 Ibid.
126 Ibid., 244.
127 Levine, 9.
128 Allende, *My Invented Country*, 172–173.
129 Allende, *Paula*, 244.
130 Ibid.
131 Ibid., 245–246.
132 Ibid., 246.
133 Ibid., 249.
134 Ibid., 250.
135 Ibid., 261.
136 Rodden, 183.
137 Allende, *Paula*, 275.
138 Ibid., 272.
139 Ibid., 275.
140 Ibid.
141 Ibid.
142 Ibid.
143 Ibid., 277.

Chapter 8

144 Karen Castellucci Cox, *Isabel Allende, A Critical Companion* (Westport, Conn.: Greenwood Press, 2003), 5.
145 Allende, *Paula*, 278.
146 Ibid.
147 Ibid., 279.
148 Ibid., 280.
149 Quoted in Zapata, 58.
150 Ibid., 59.
151 Allende, *Paula*, 287.
152 Ibid.
153 Ibid., 288.
154 Cox, 6.
155 Allende, *Paula*, 296.
156 Ibid., 298.
157 Ibid.
158 Ibid., 299.
159 Ibid.
160 Ibid.
161 Ibid., 300.
162 Ibid., 302.
163 Rodden, 193.
164 Cox, 12.
165 Allende, *Paula*, 312–313.
166 Ibid., 313.

Chapter 9

167 Ibid., 20.
168 Ibid., 3.
169 Rodden, 25.
170 Zapata, 136.
171 Allende, *My Invented Country*, 197.
172 Ibid., 197–198.

Bibliography

Allende, Isabel. *My Invented Country, A Memoir*. New York: Perennial, 2004.

——. *Paula*. New York: HarperCollins Publishers, 1994.

Bloom, Harold, ed. *Bloom's Modern Critical Views: Isabel Allende*. Philadelphia: Chelsea House Publishers, 2003.

Cox, Karen Castellucci. *Isabel Allende, A Critical Companion*. Westport, Conn.: Greenwood Press, 2003.

Feal, Rosemary G., and Yvette E. Miller. *Isabel Allende Today: An Anthology of Essays*. Pittsburgh, Pa.: Latin American Literary Review Press, 2002.

Hart, Patricia. *Narrative Magic in the Fiction of Isabel Allende*. Cranbury, N.J.: Associated University Presses, 1989.

Levine, Linda Gould. *Isabel Allende*. New York: Twayne Publishers, 2002.

Lindsay, Claire. *Locating Latin American Women Writers*. New York: Peter Lang Publishing, Inc., 2003.

Rodden, John, ed. *Conversations with Isabel Allende*. Austin, Tex.: University of Texas Press, 1999.

Skidmore, Thomas, and Peter Smith. "Chile, Democracy, Socialism, and Repression." *Modern Latin America*, ed. Thomas Skidmore and Peter Smith. New York: Oxford University Press, 1984.

Zapata, Celia Correas. *Isabel Allende: Life and Spirits*. Houston, Tex.: Arte Publico Press, 2002.

Books by Isabel Allende (English Versions)

Aphrodite: A Memoir of the Senses. New York: HarperCollins, 1998.

Daughter of Fortune. New York: HarperCollins Publishers, 2001.

Eva Luna. New York: Knopf Publishing Group, 1988.

Forest of the Pygmies. New York: HarperCollins Publishers, 2005.

The House of the Spirits. New York: Knopf Publishing Group, 1985.

The Infinite Plan. New York: HarperCollins Publishers, 1993.

Kingdom of the Golden Dragon. New York: HarperCollins Publishers, 2005.

Of Love and Shadows. New York: Bantam Books, 1988.

Portrait in Sepia. New York: HarperCollins Publishers, 2002

The Stories of Eva Luna. New York: Simon & Schuster Adult Publishing Group, 1991.

Zorro: A Novel. New York: HarperCollins Publishers, 2005.

Further Reading

Main, Mary. *Isabel Allende: Award-Winning Latin American Author.* Berkeley Heights, NJ: Enslow Publishers, Inc., 2005.

Marvis, Barbara. *Famous People of Hispanic Heritage*, Vol. *8.* Childs, MD: Mitchell Lane Publishers, Inc., 1997.

Osborne, Melissa. *Isabel Allende.* San Diego: Thomson Gale Group, 1996.

Web sites

Isabel Allende Bio
www.en.wikipedia.org/wiki/Isabel_Allende

HarperCollins Isabel Allende Site
http://www.harpercollins.co.uk/authors/default.aspx?id=136

Isabel Allende Official Site
www.isabelallende.com

Isabel Allende Foundation
http://www.isabelallendefoundation.org/english/home.html

Isabel Allende Q&A
www.motherjones.com/arts/qa/1994/09/allende.html

Index

About the Author

Tim McNeese is associate professor of history at York College in York, Nebraska. Professor McNeese earned an Associate of Arts degree from York College, a Bachelor of Arts in History and Political Science from Harding University, and a Master of Arts in History from Southwest Missouri State University. A prolific author of books for elementary, middle and high school, and college readers, McNeese has written more than 80 books and educational materials over the past 20 years, on everything from Western wagon trains to the Space Race. His writing has earned him a citation in the library reference work *Something about the Author*. Professor McNeese appeared as a consulting historian for the History Channel program, *Risk Takers/History Makers: John Wesley Powell and the Grand Canyon*. His wife, Beverly, is assistant professor of English at York College. They have two children, Noah and Summer. Readers are encouraged to contact Professor McNeese at tdmcneese@york.edu.

Picture Credits